Mandalas
Only for women

1st edition 2021.
Copyright © 2021 by Mandal Design.
ISBN: 9798593362513
© Copyright por Mandal Design.

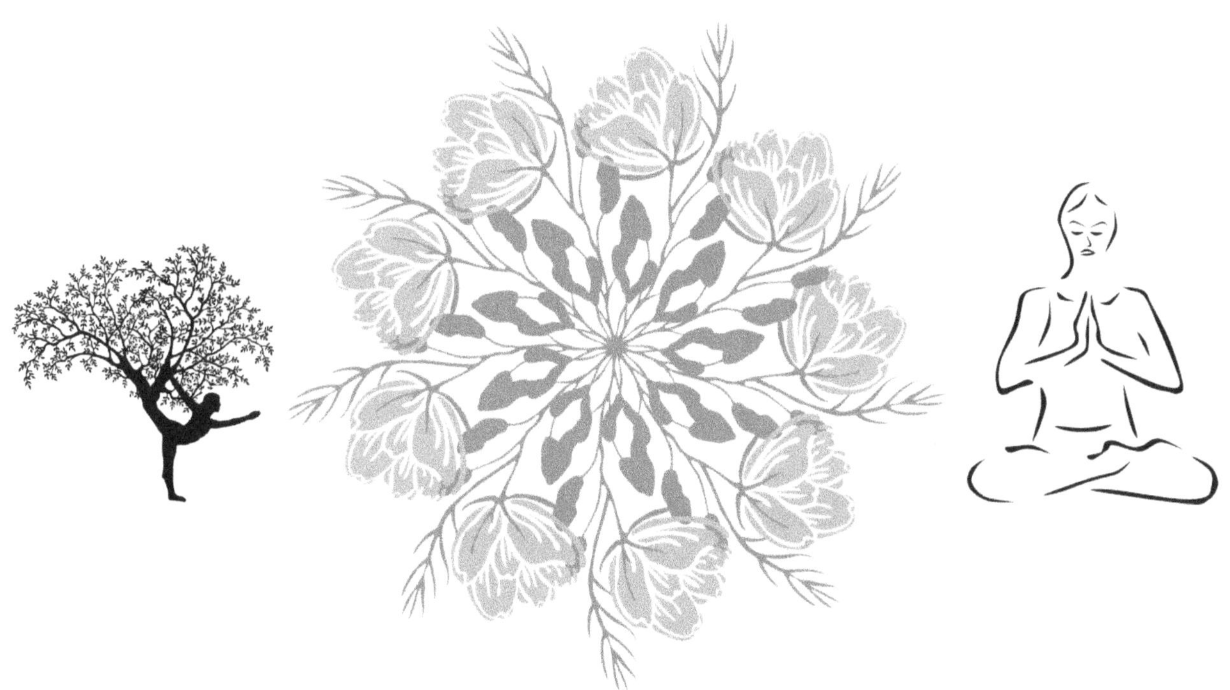

This edition has been elaborated specially for women, being an expression of the soul, it harmonizes our inner world with the outside. By awakening the senses, it stimulates creativity.

Mandalas are an excellent activity for any woman who needs a bit of calm or wants to spend time with herself and have fun creating.

They help you develop patience, awaken the senses and intuition, help you express yourself, relax, connect with our feelings and expose them through colors.

It is an excellent tool for coordination, expression and mental development. It will improve concentration and self-control.

Enjoy it!

By Mandal Design

This book belongs to:

____

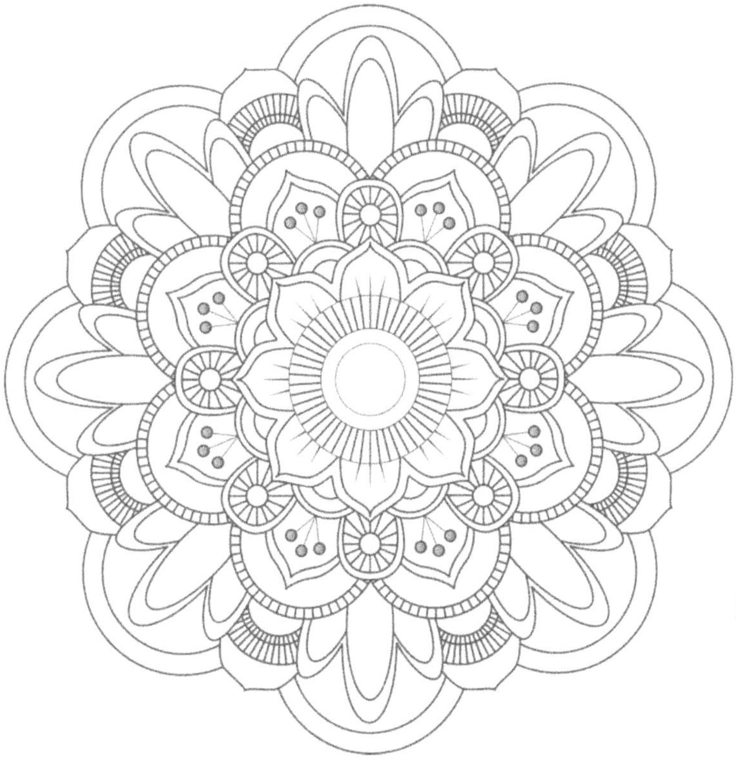

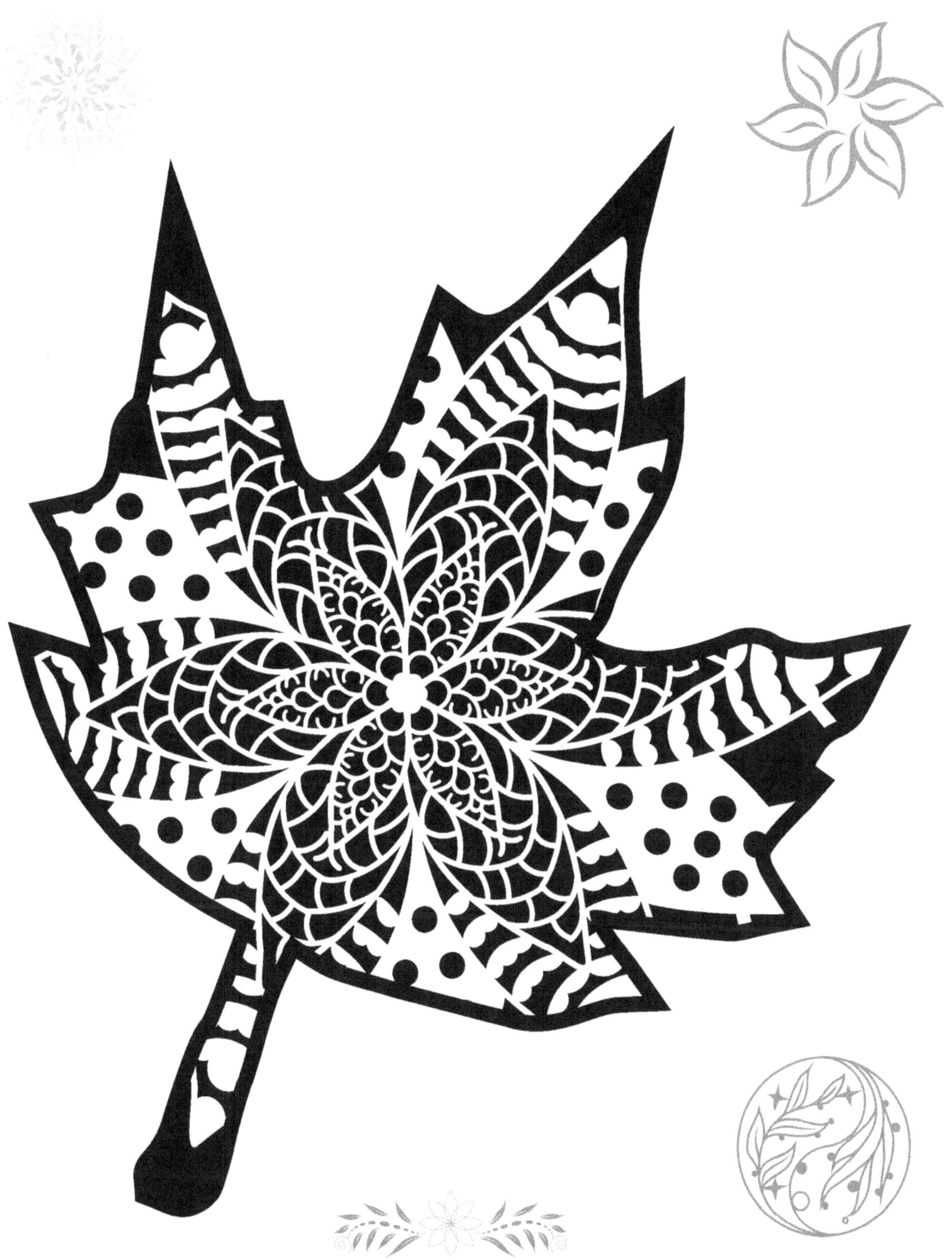

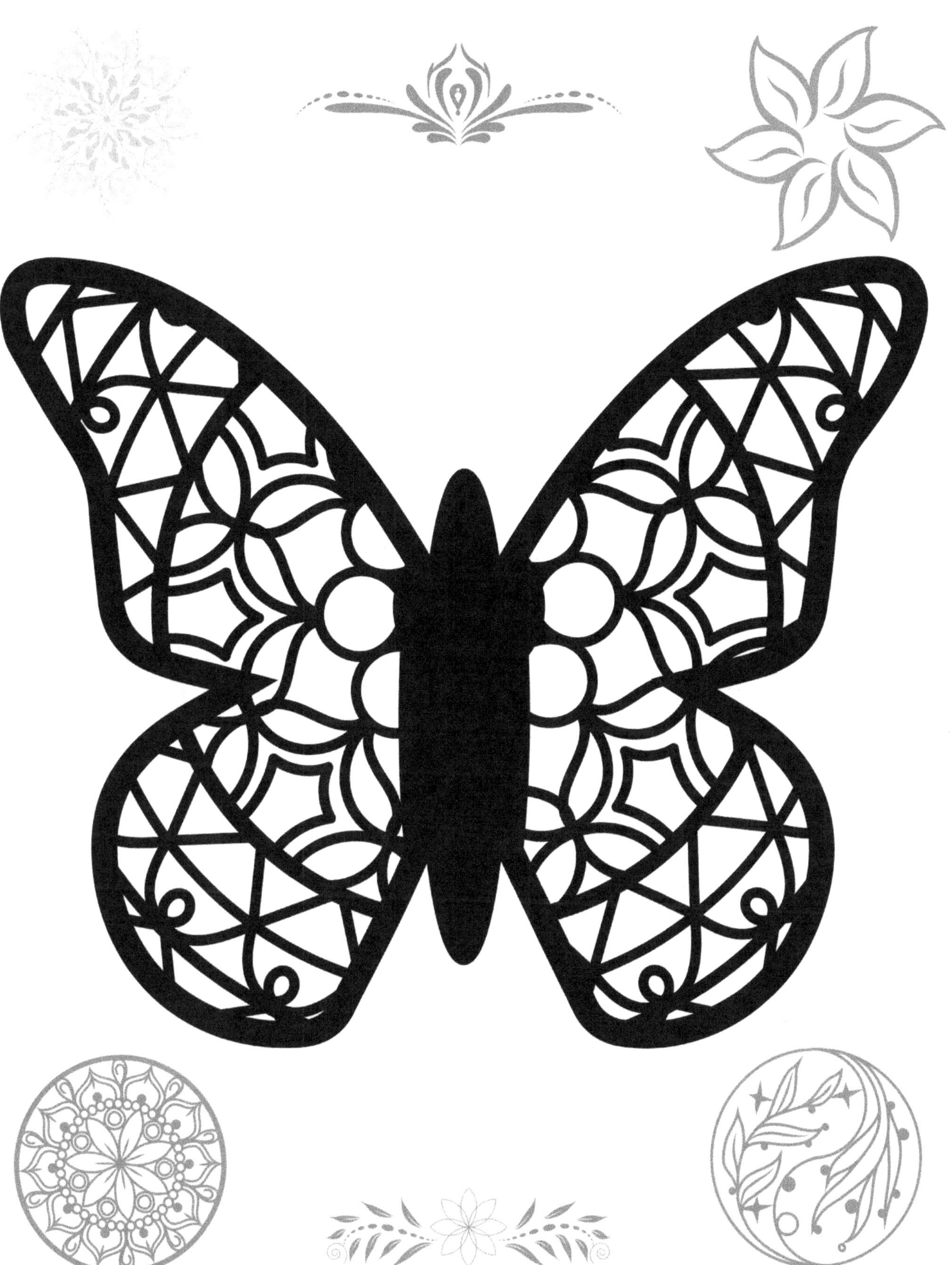

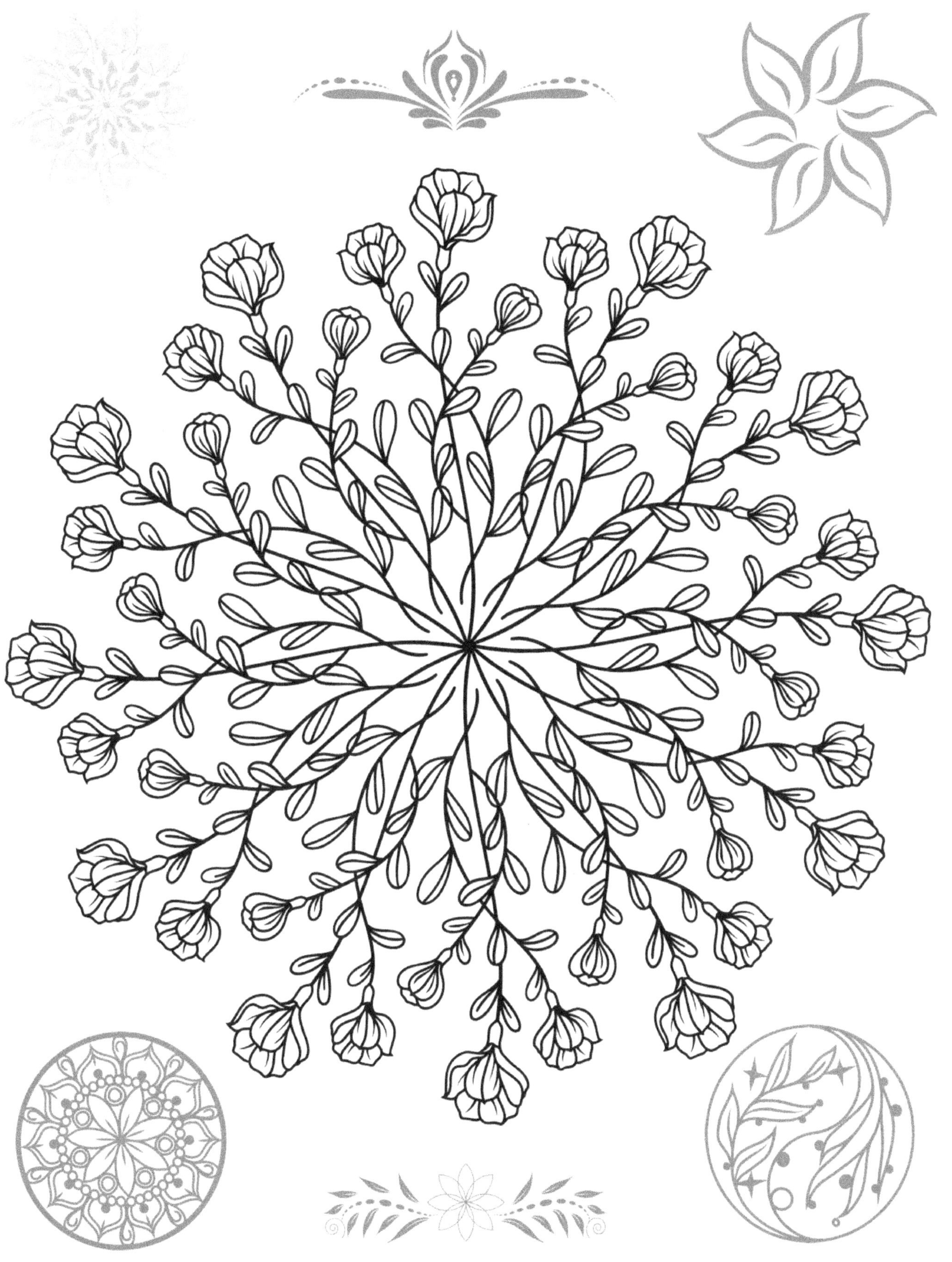

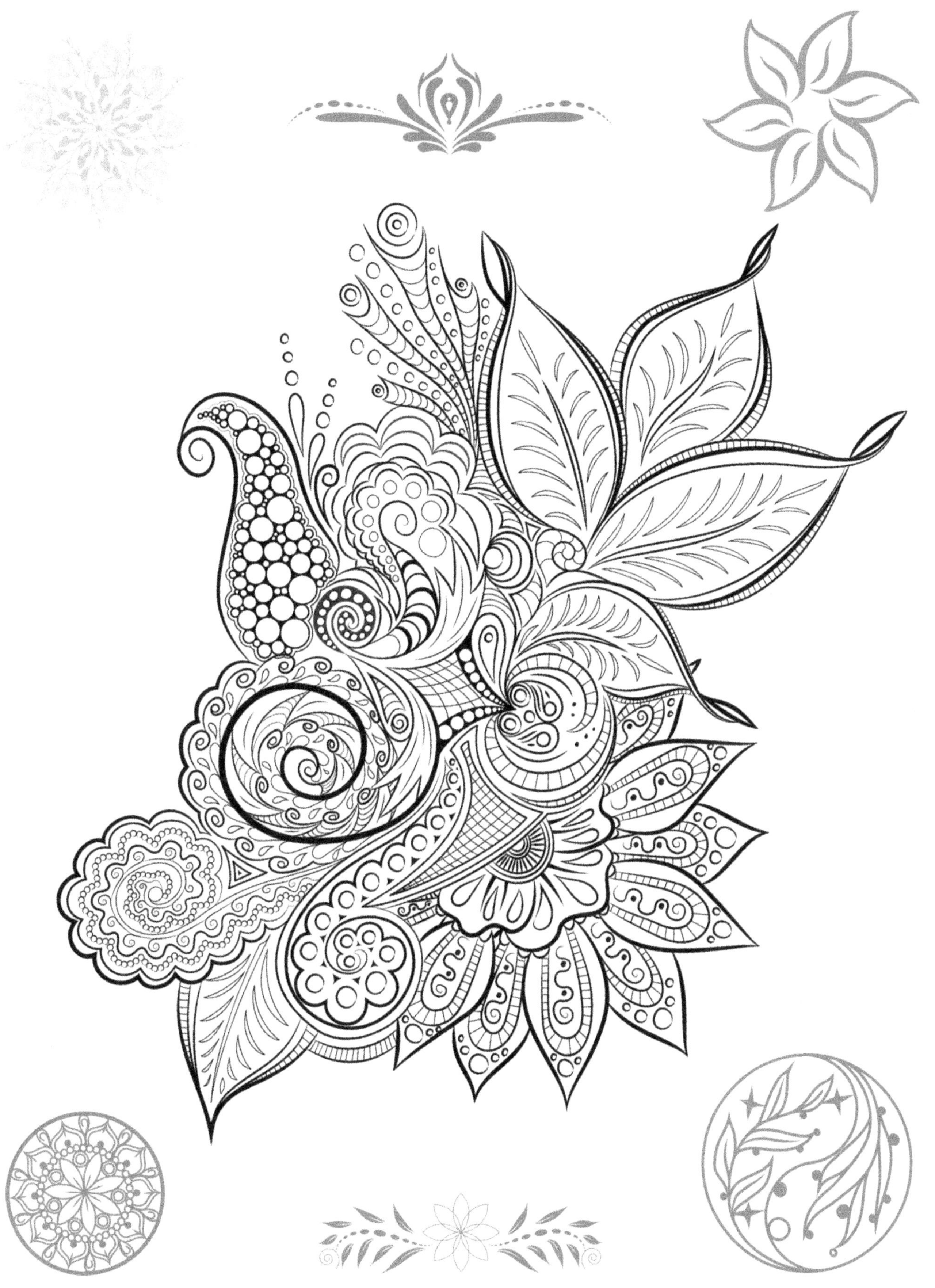

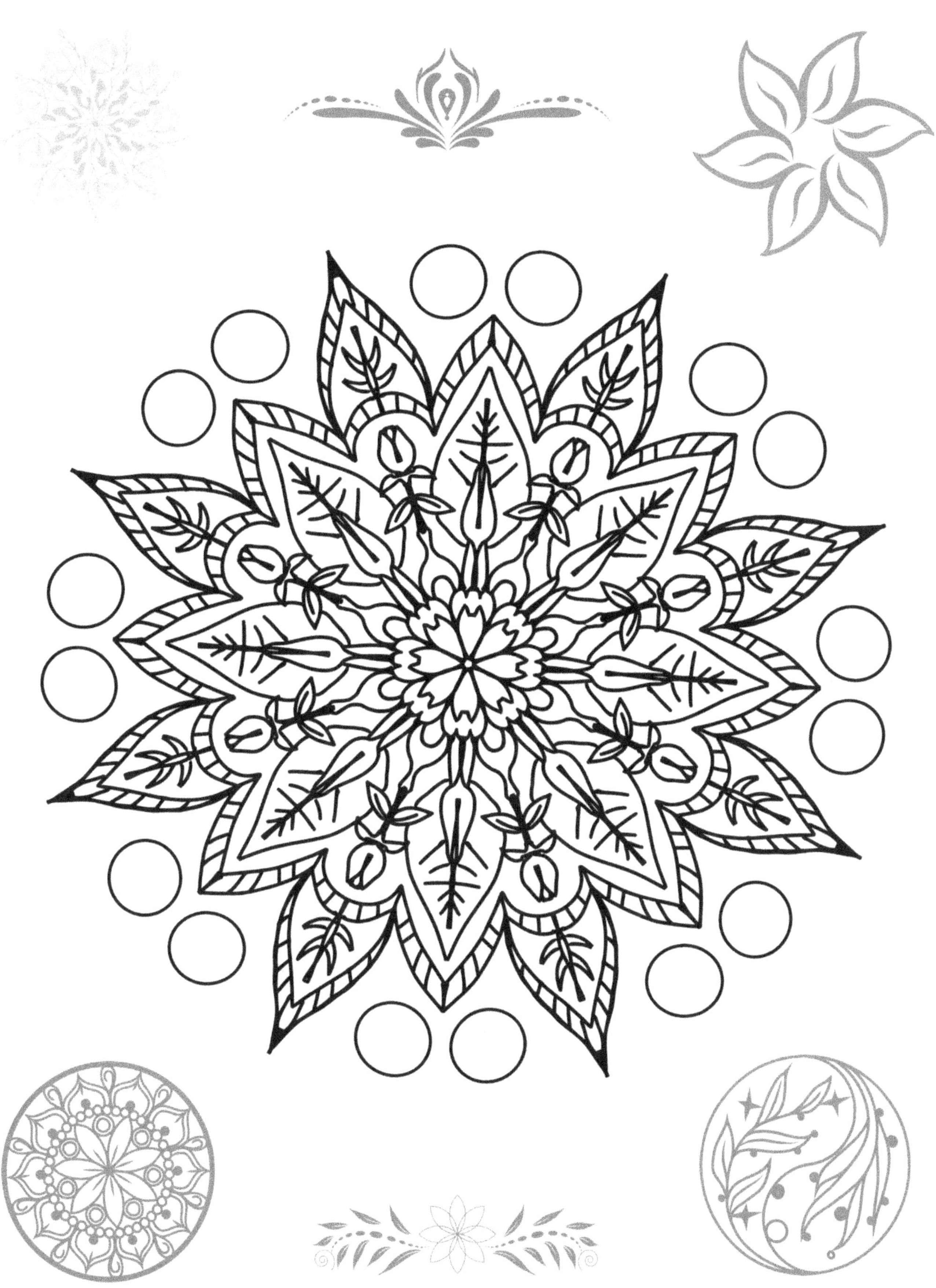

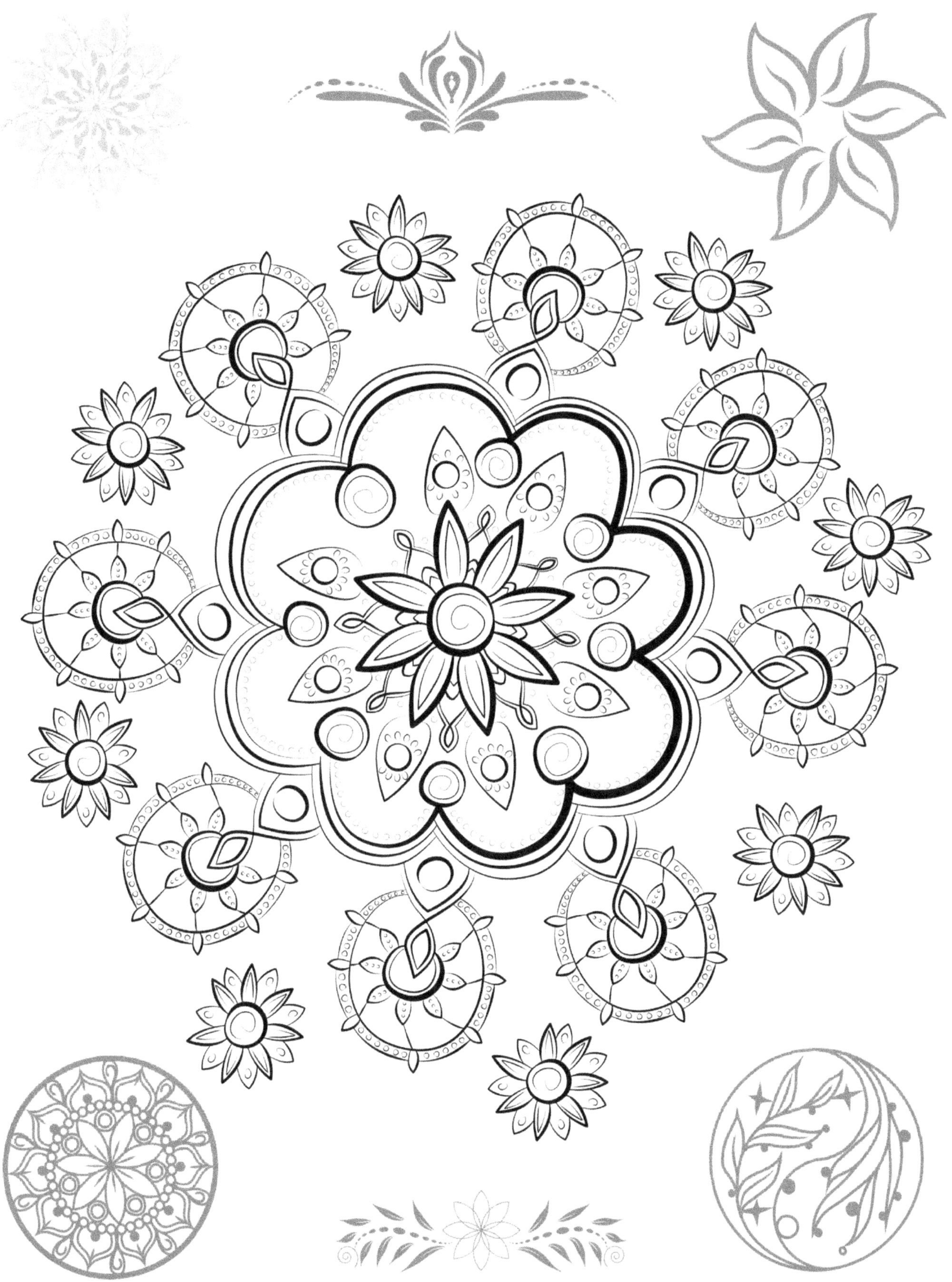

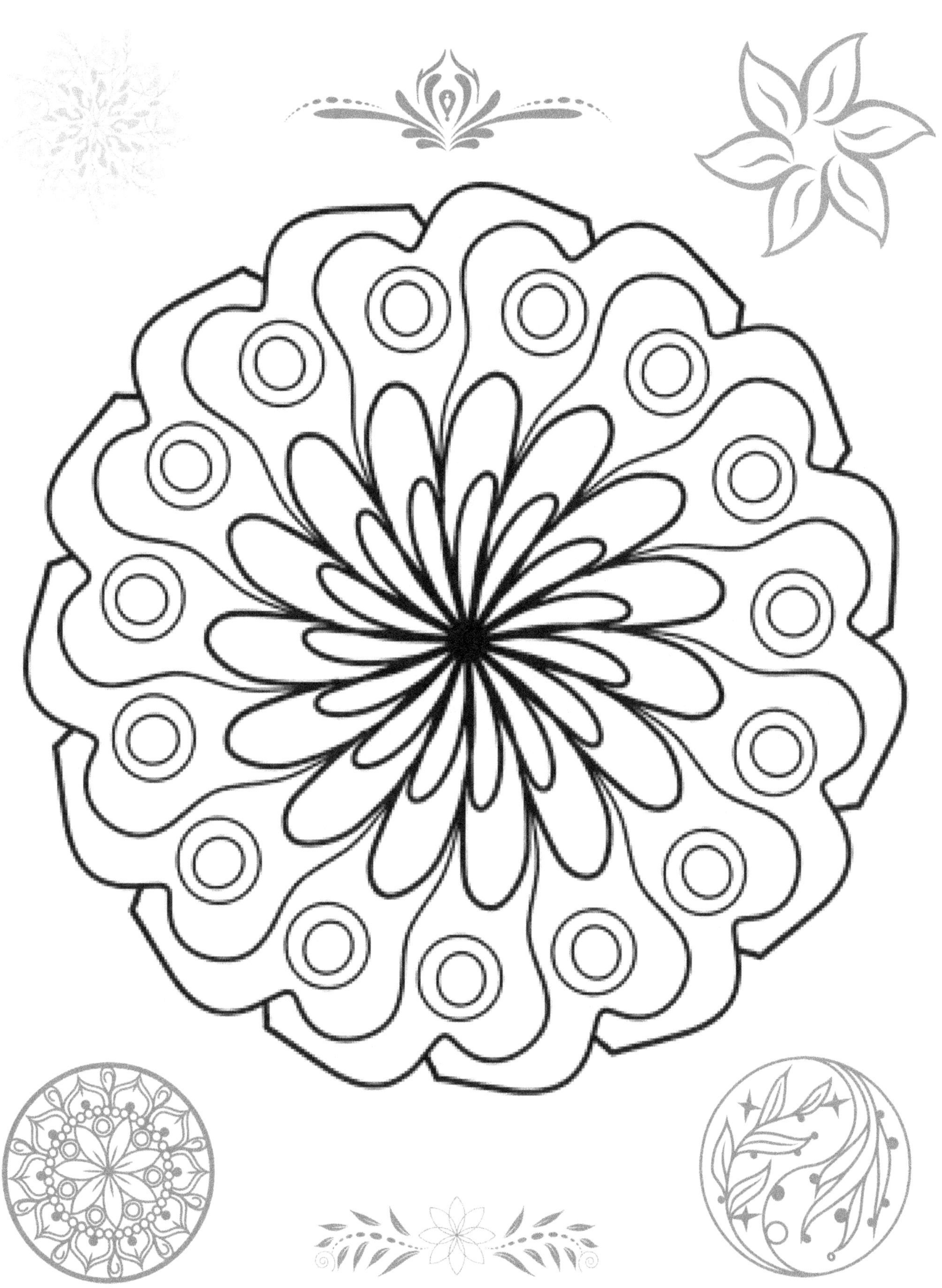

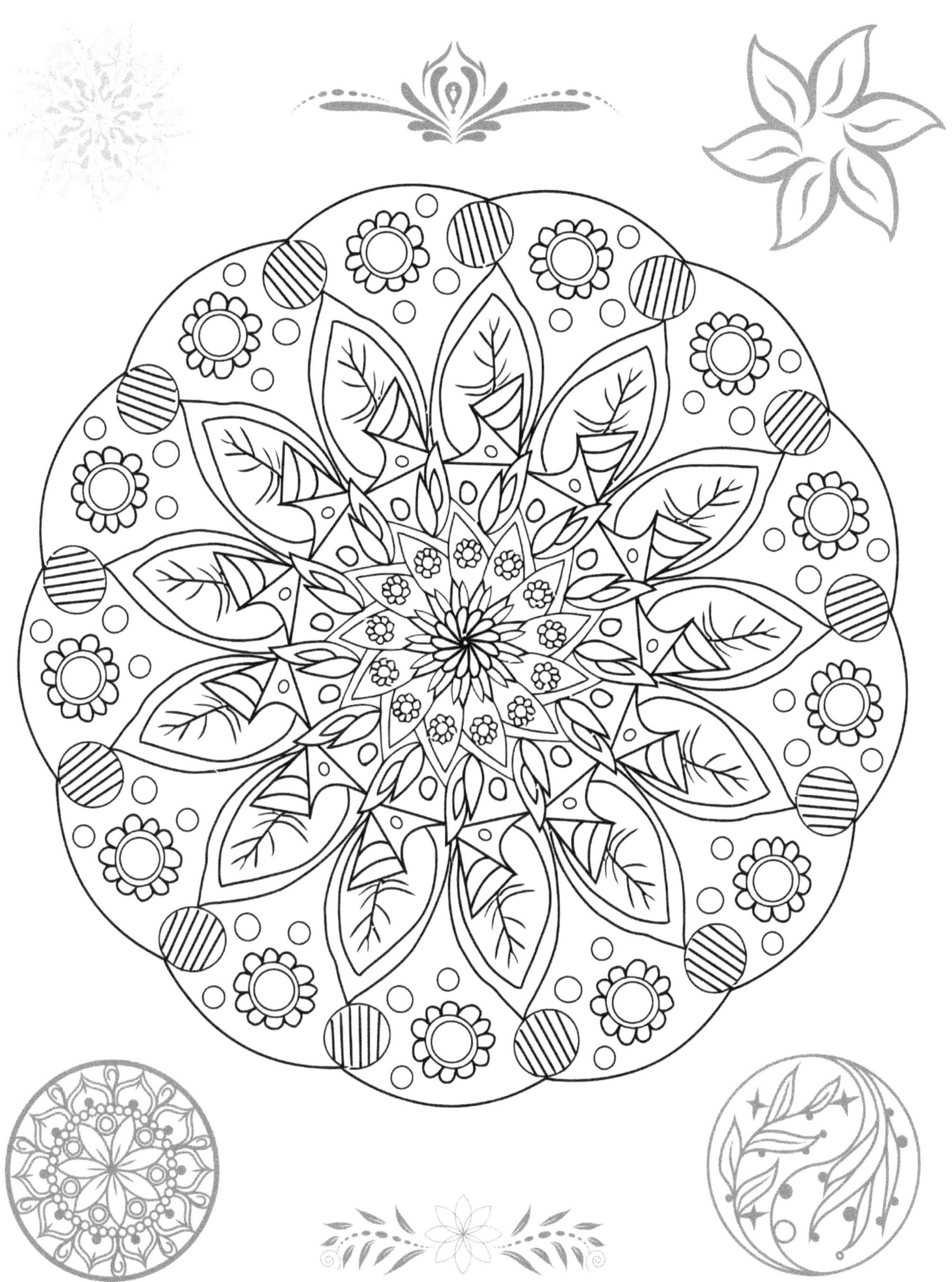

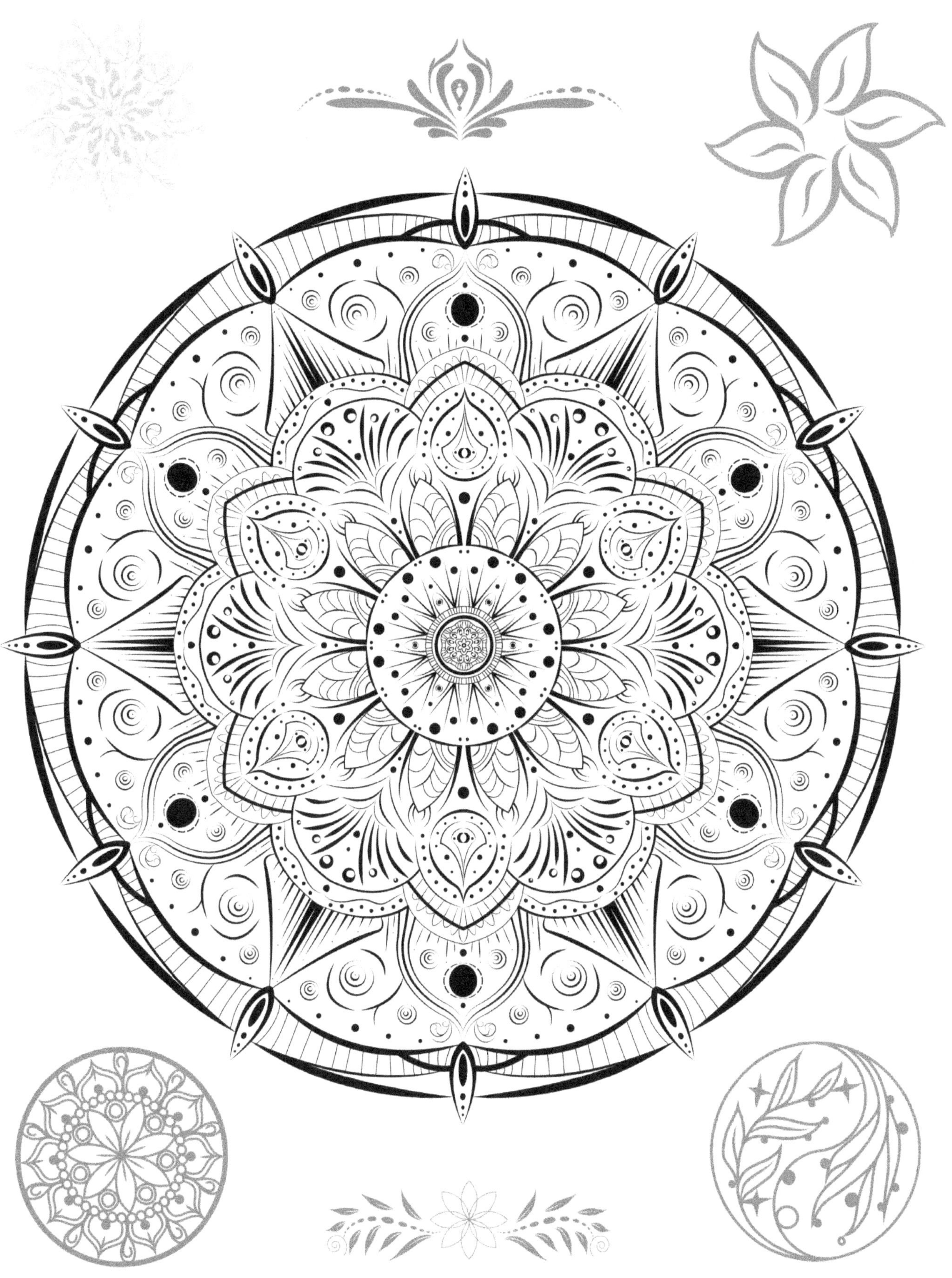

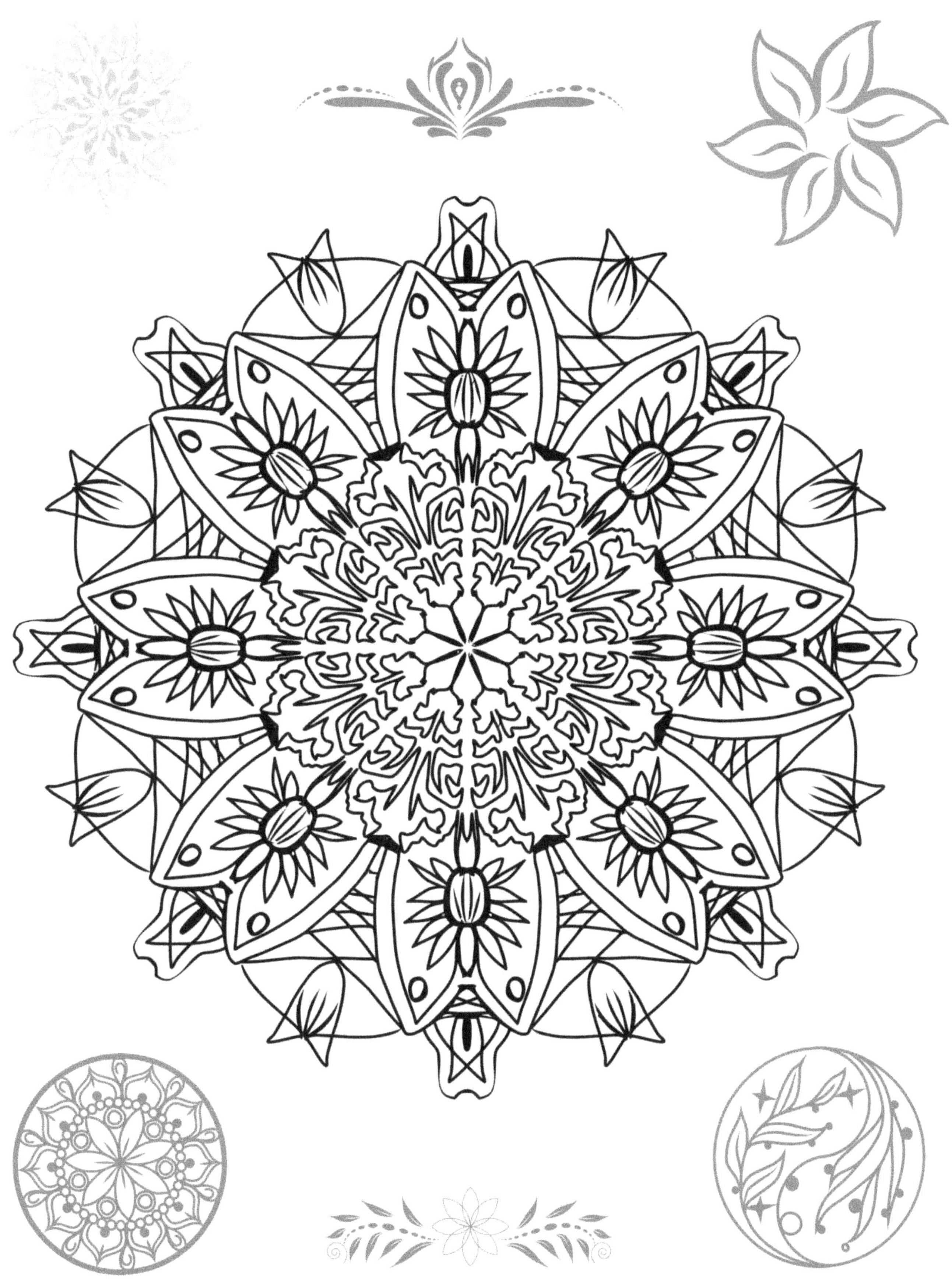

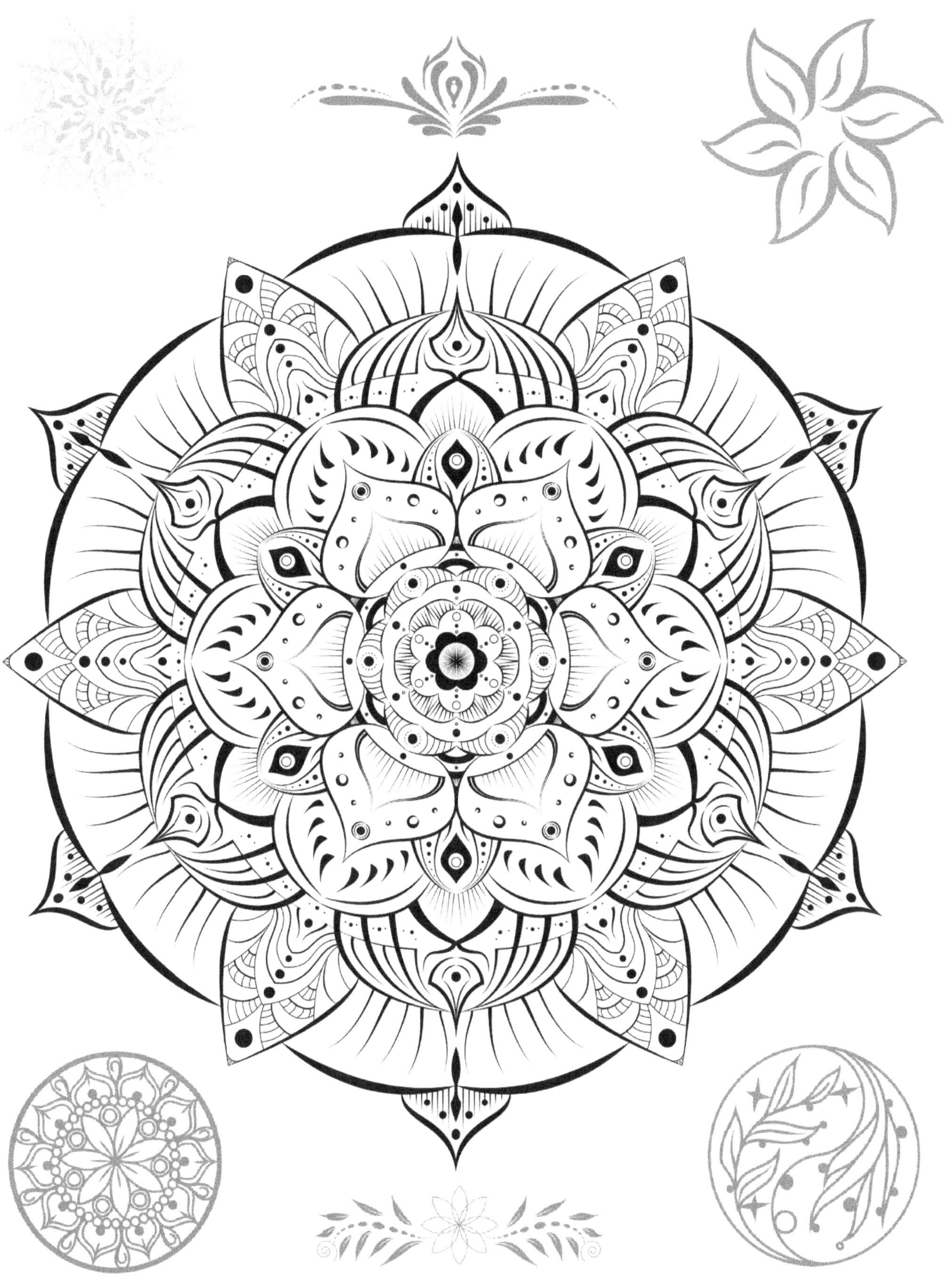

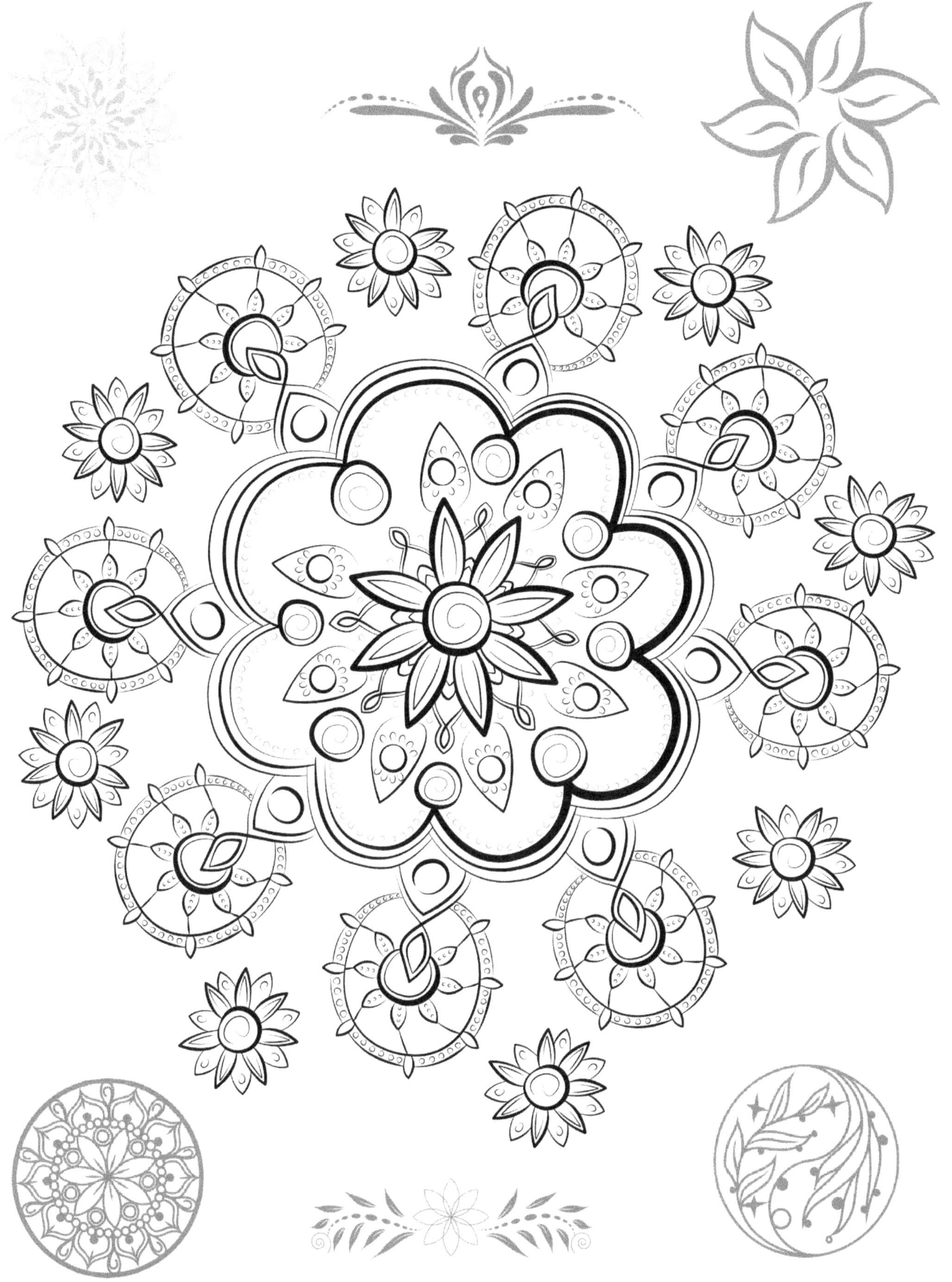

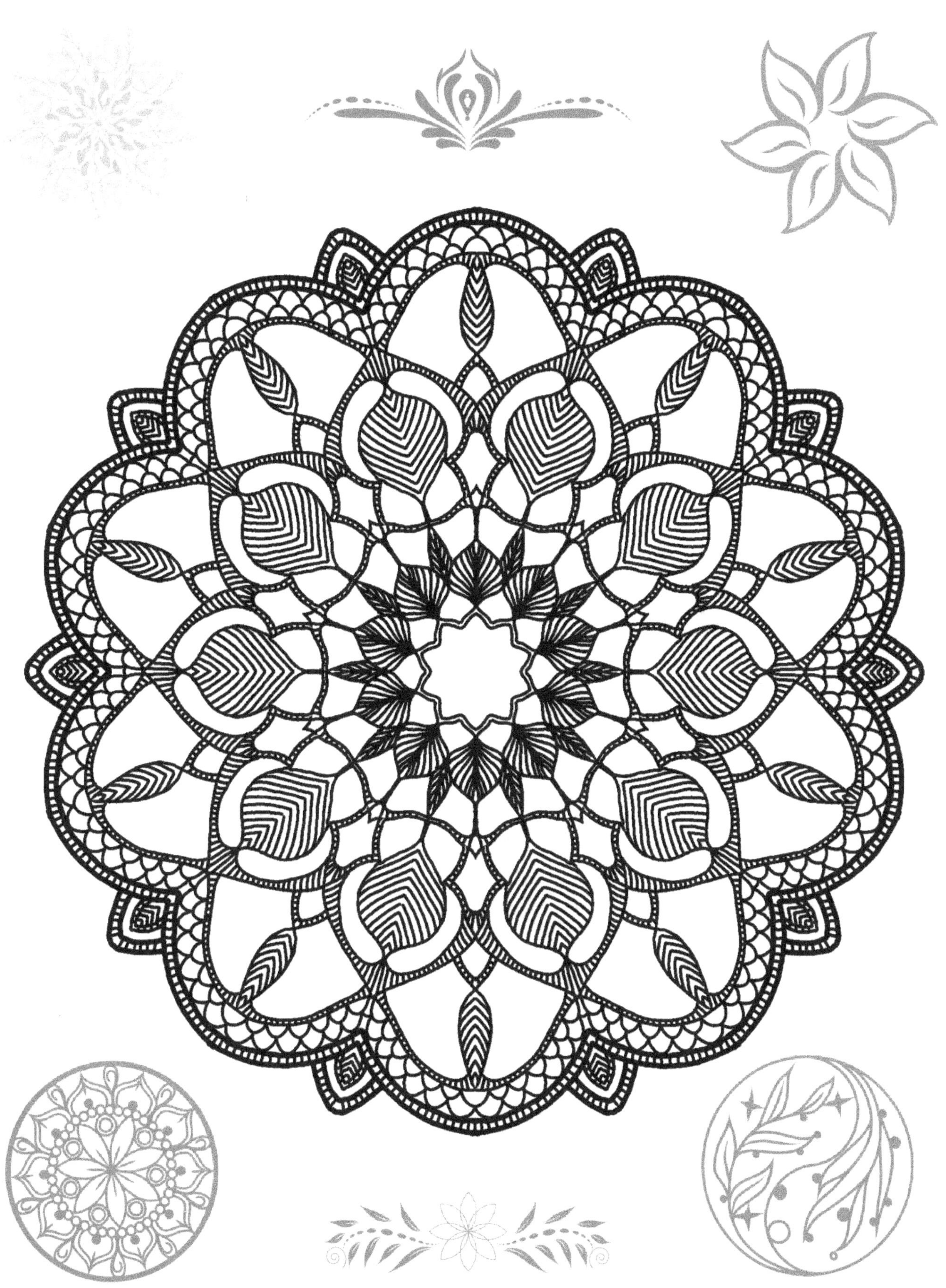

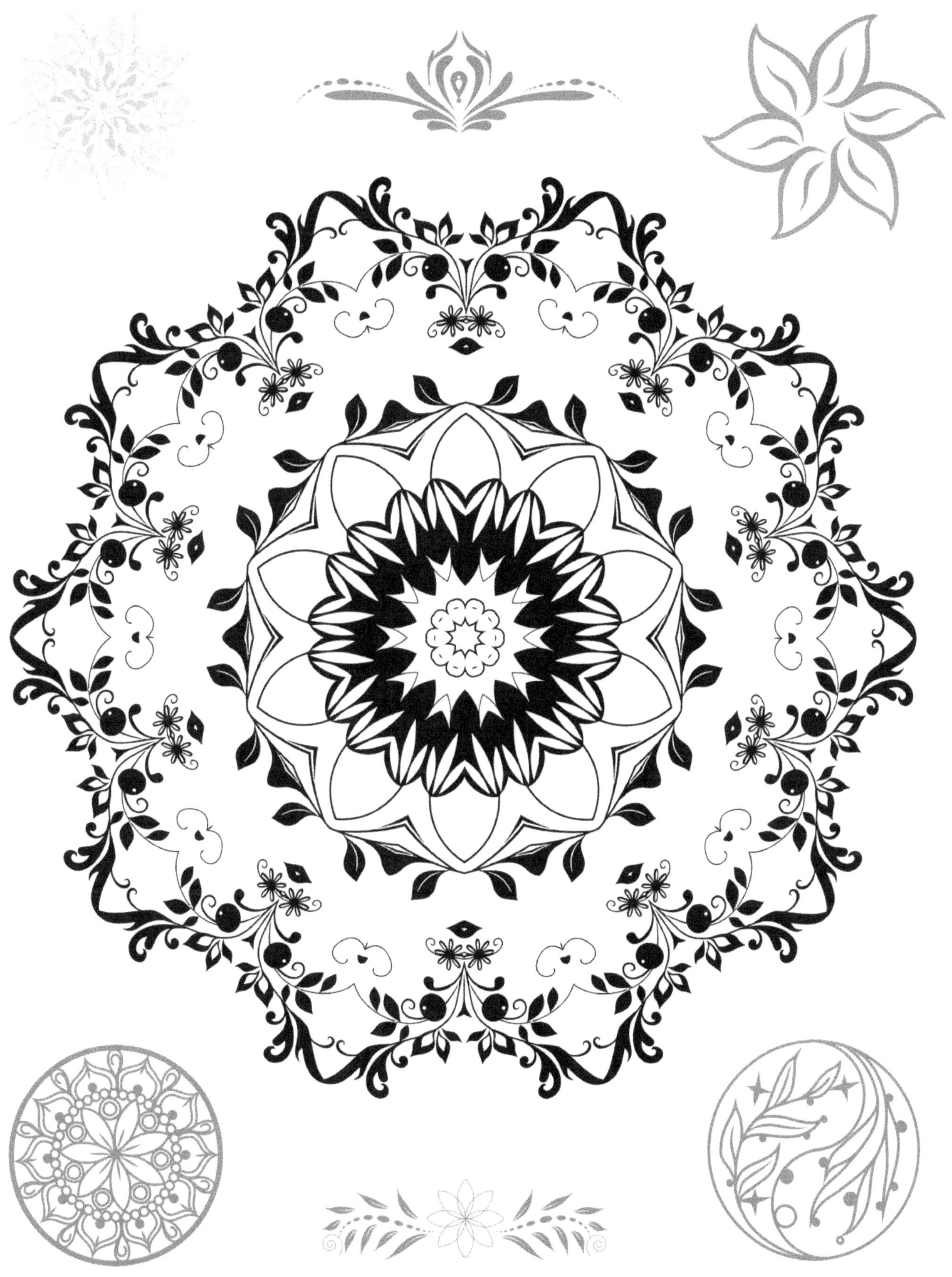

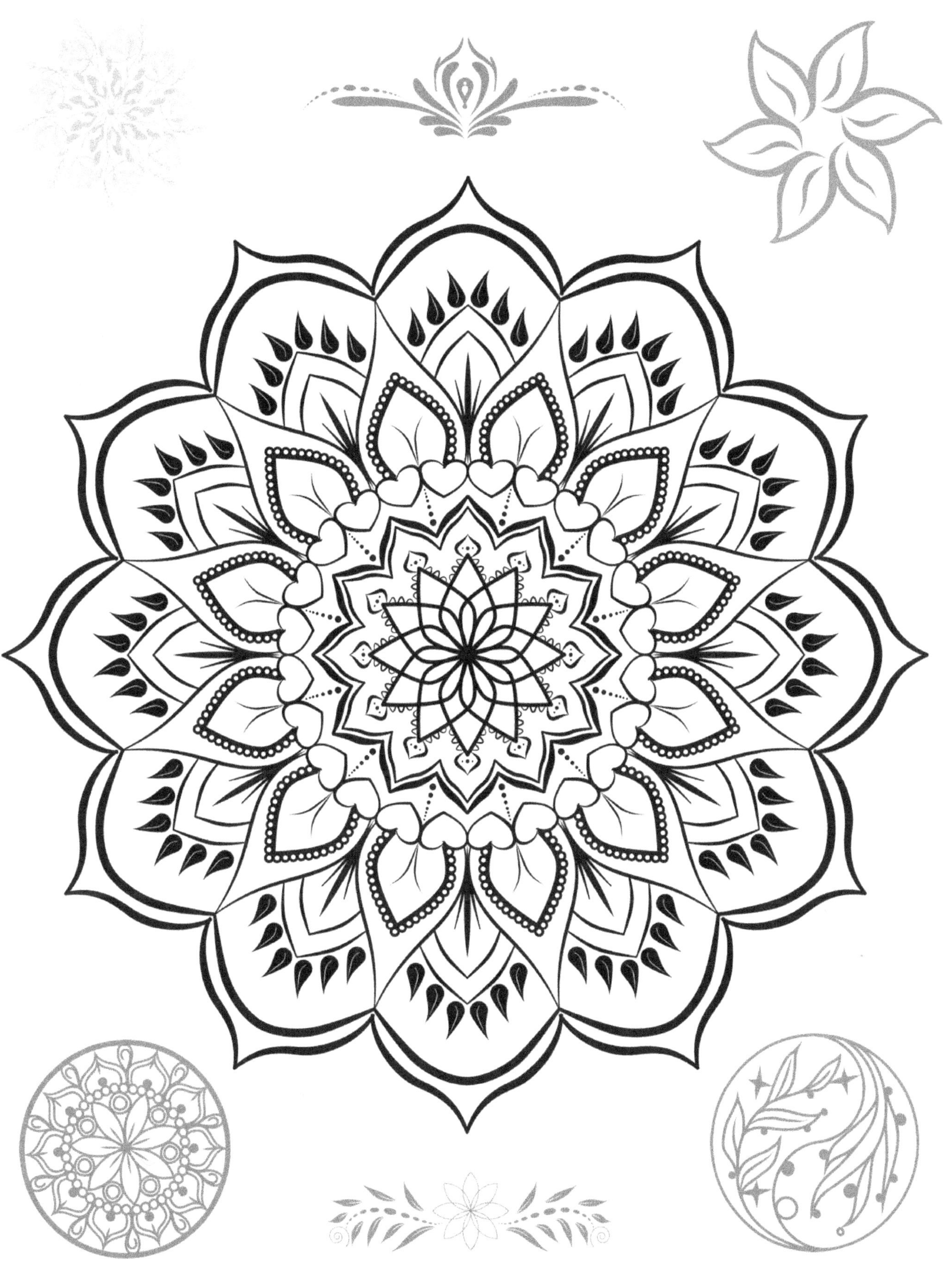

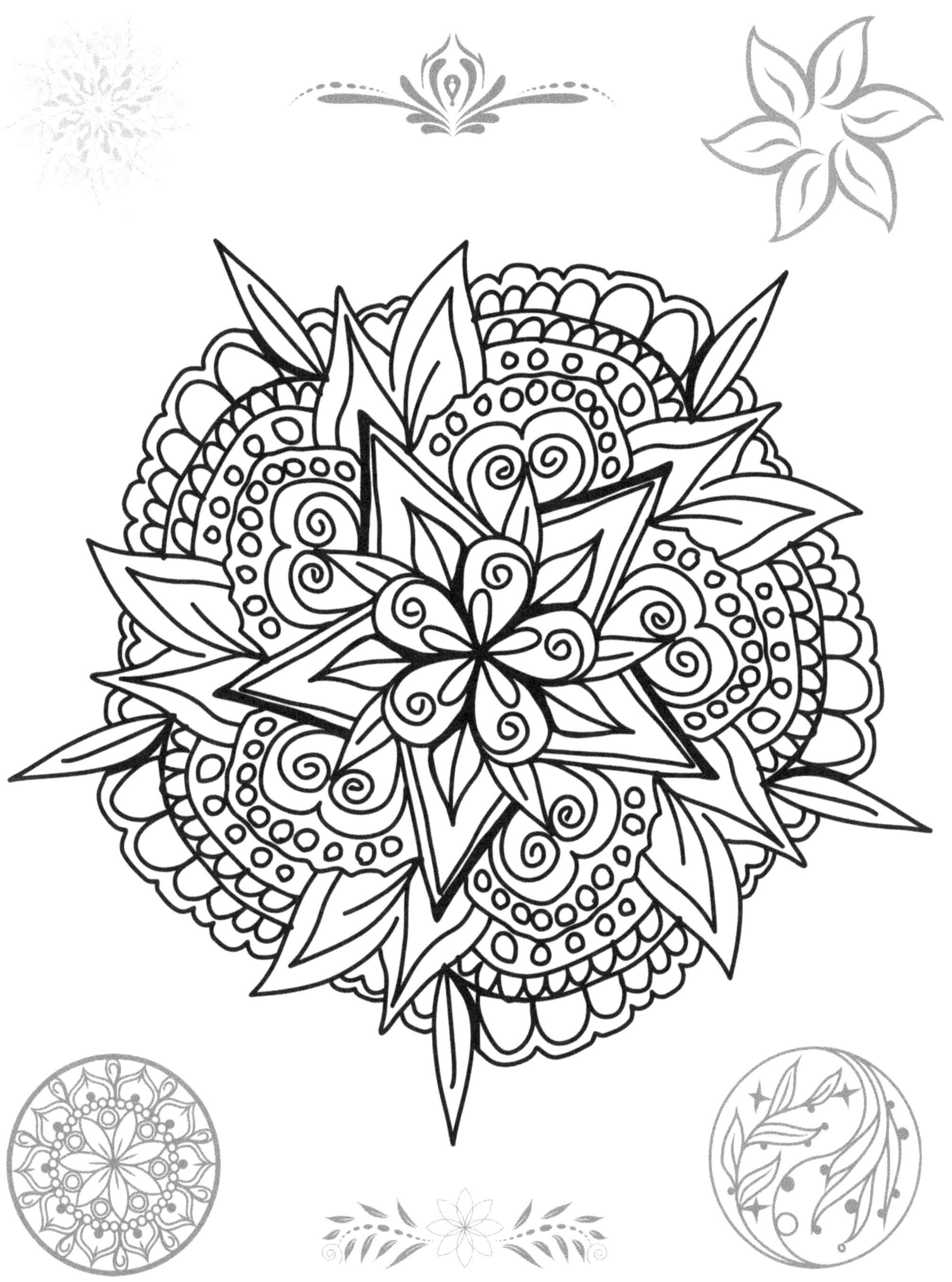

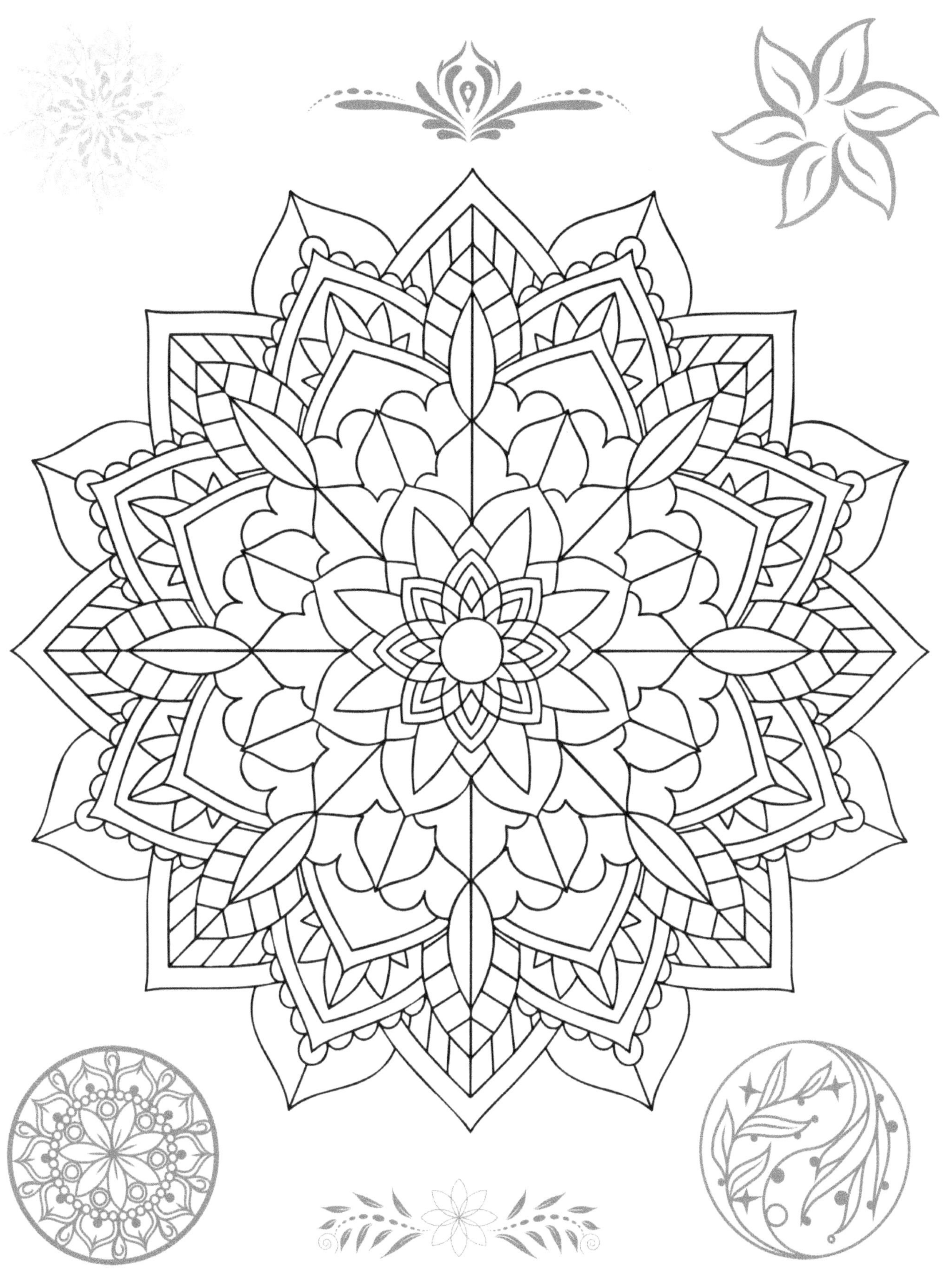

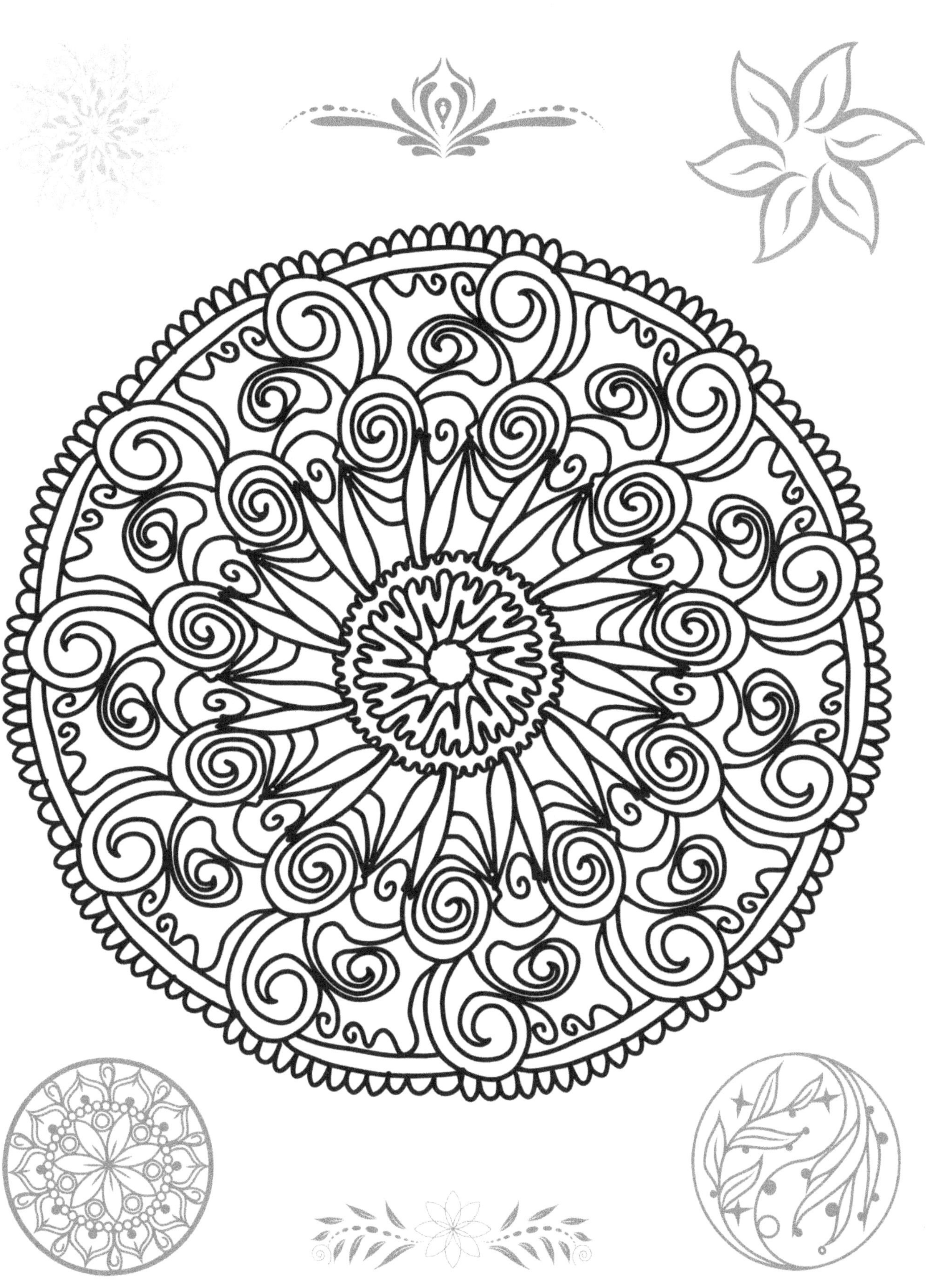

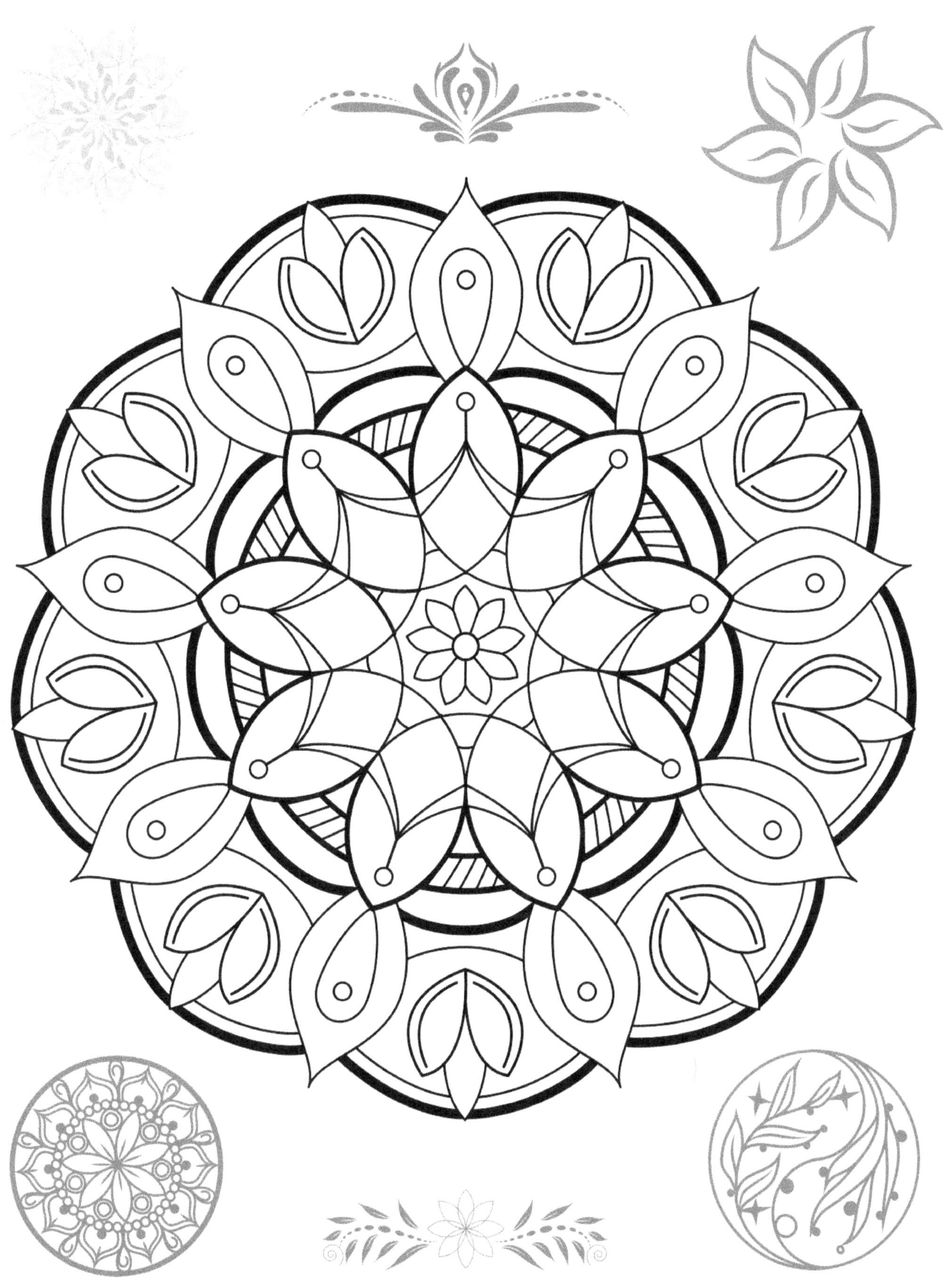

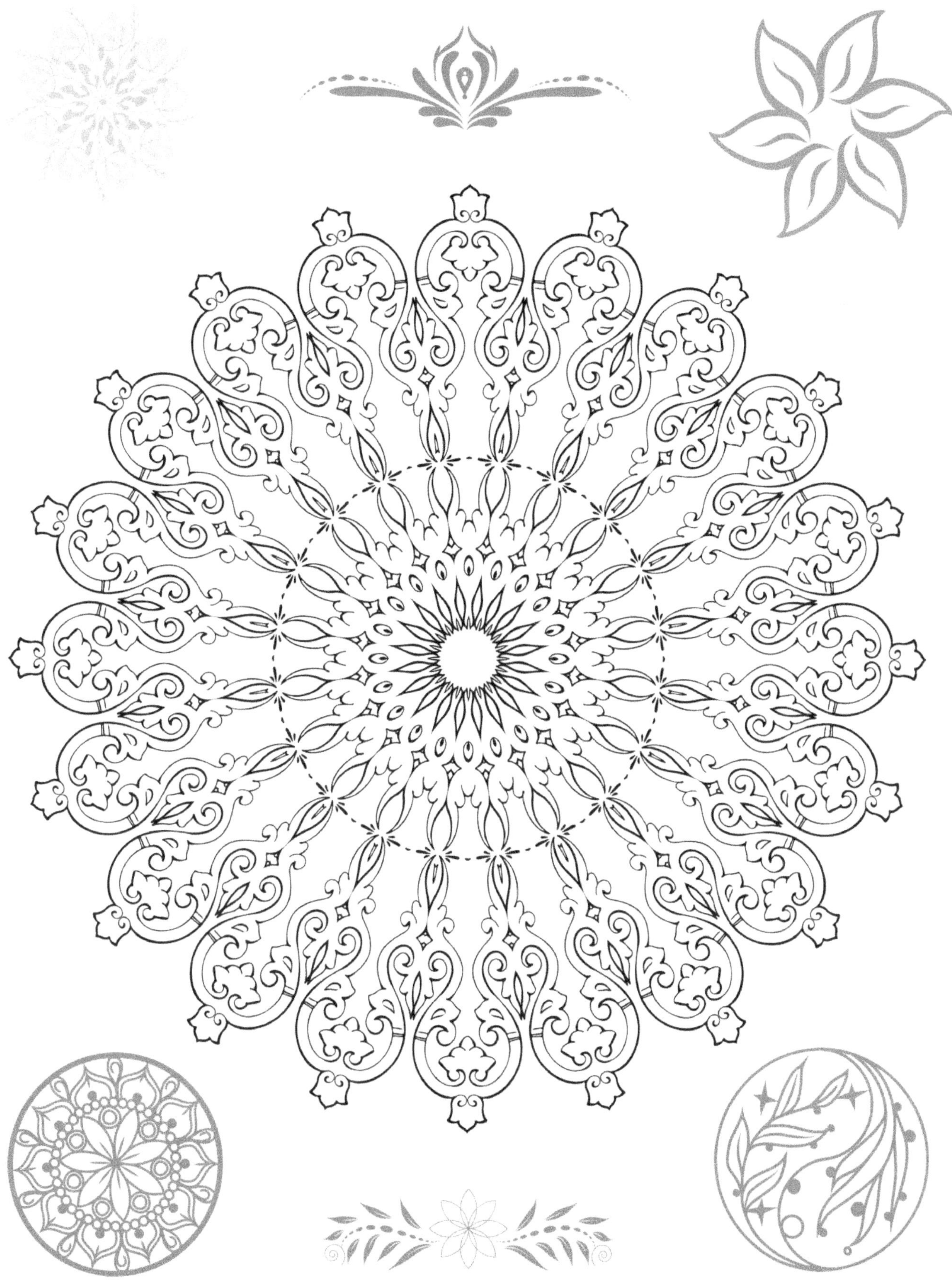

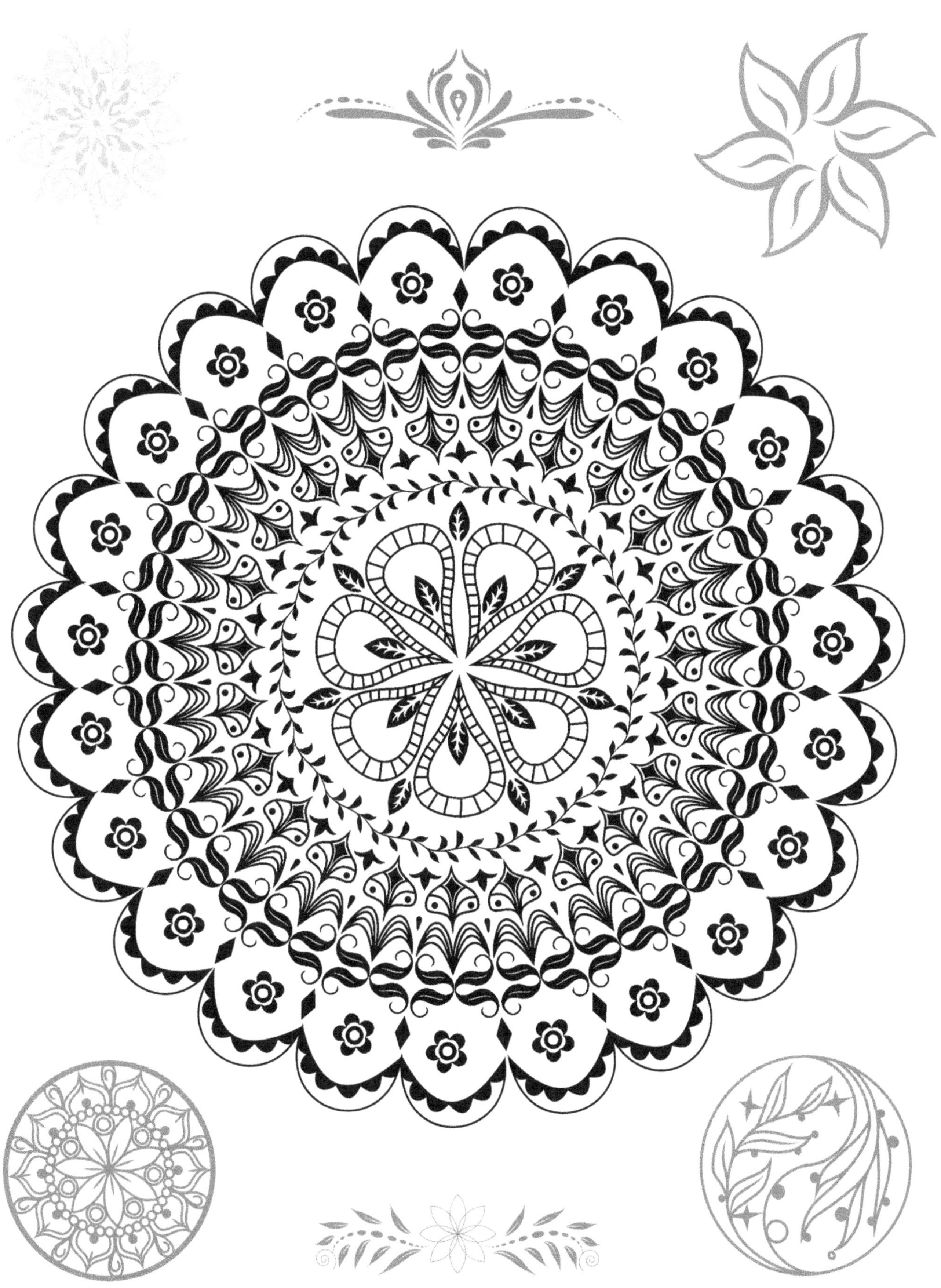

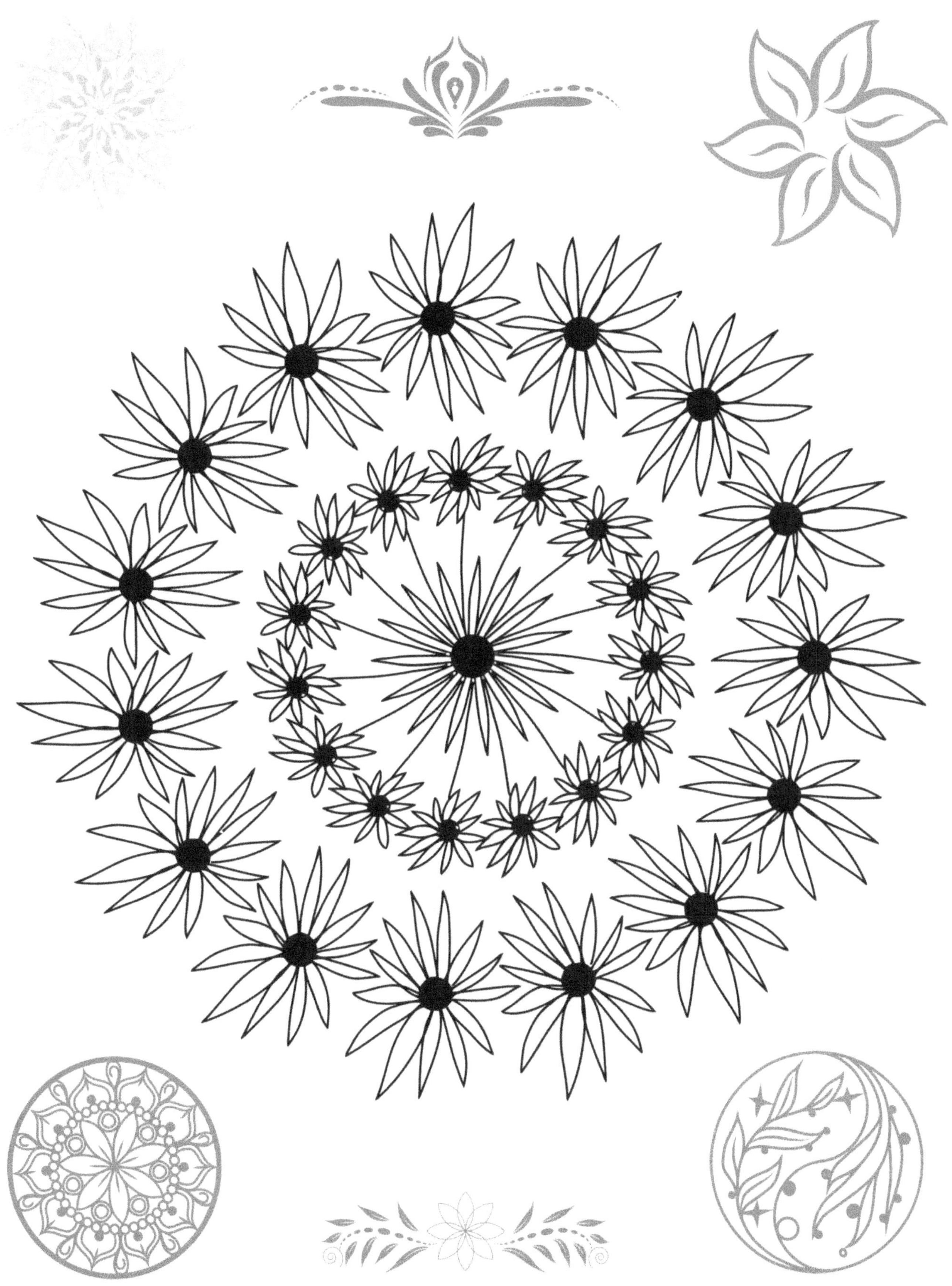

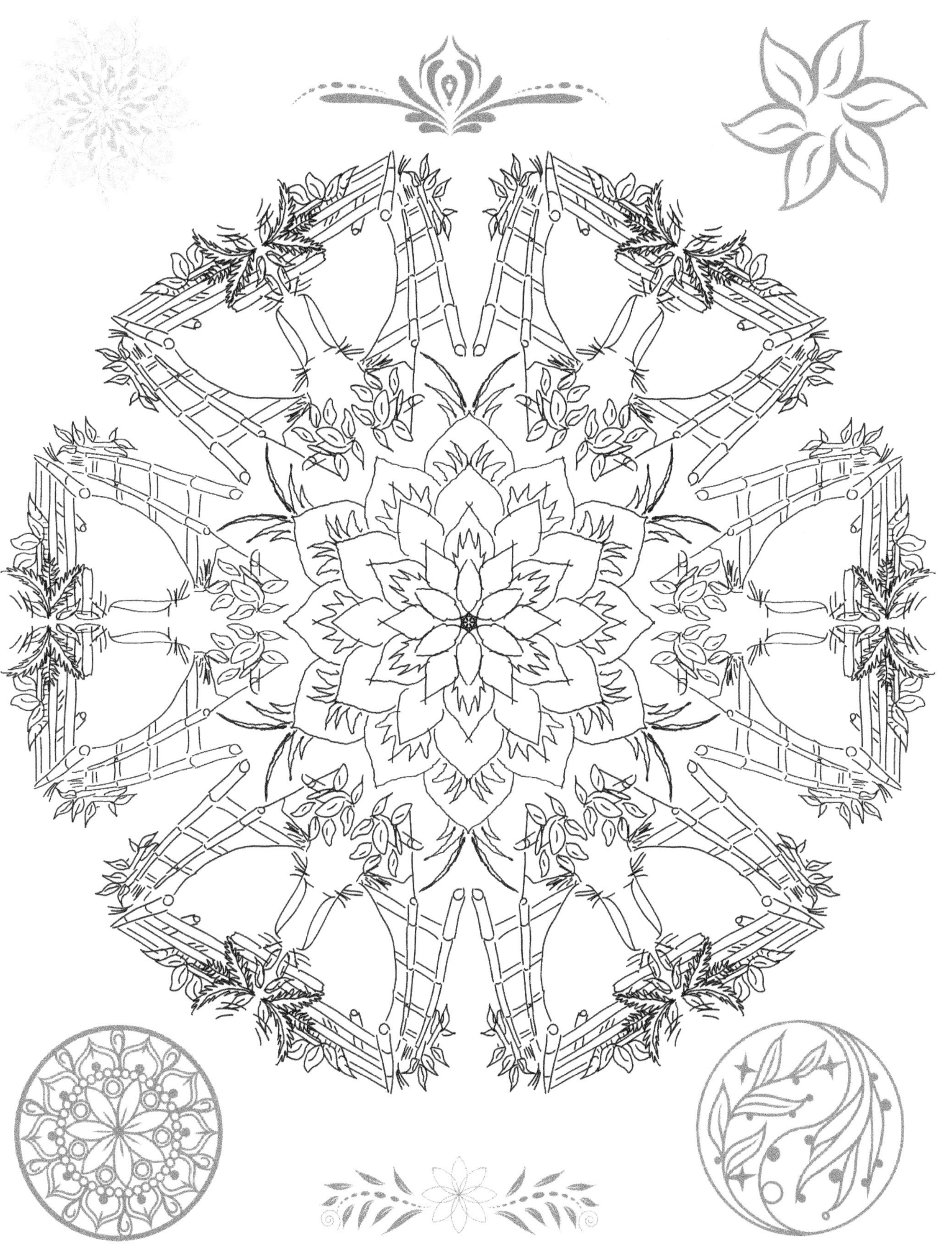

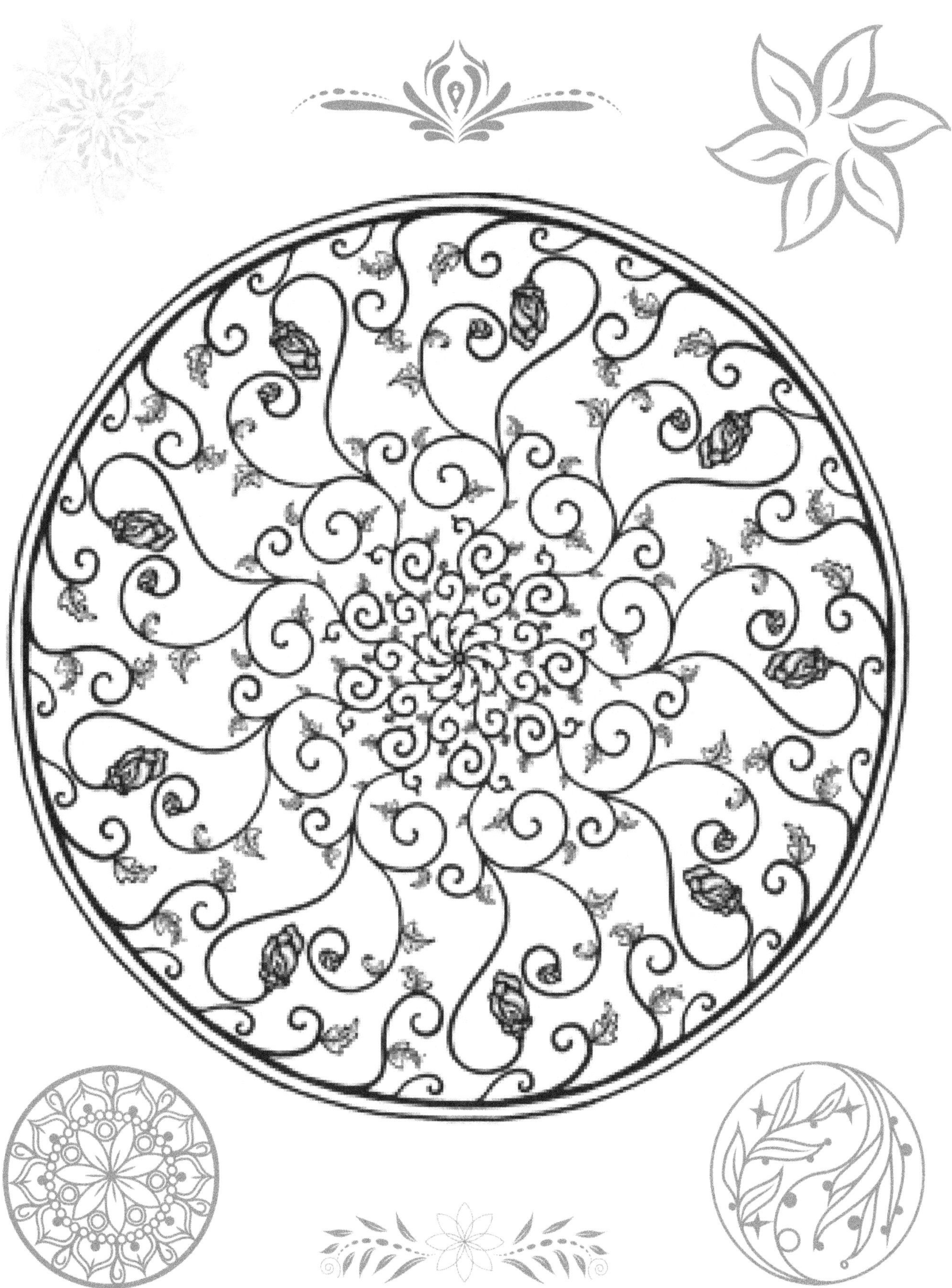

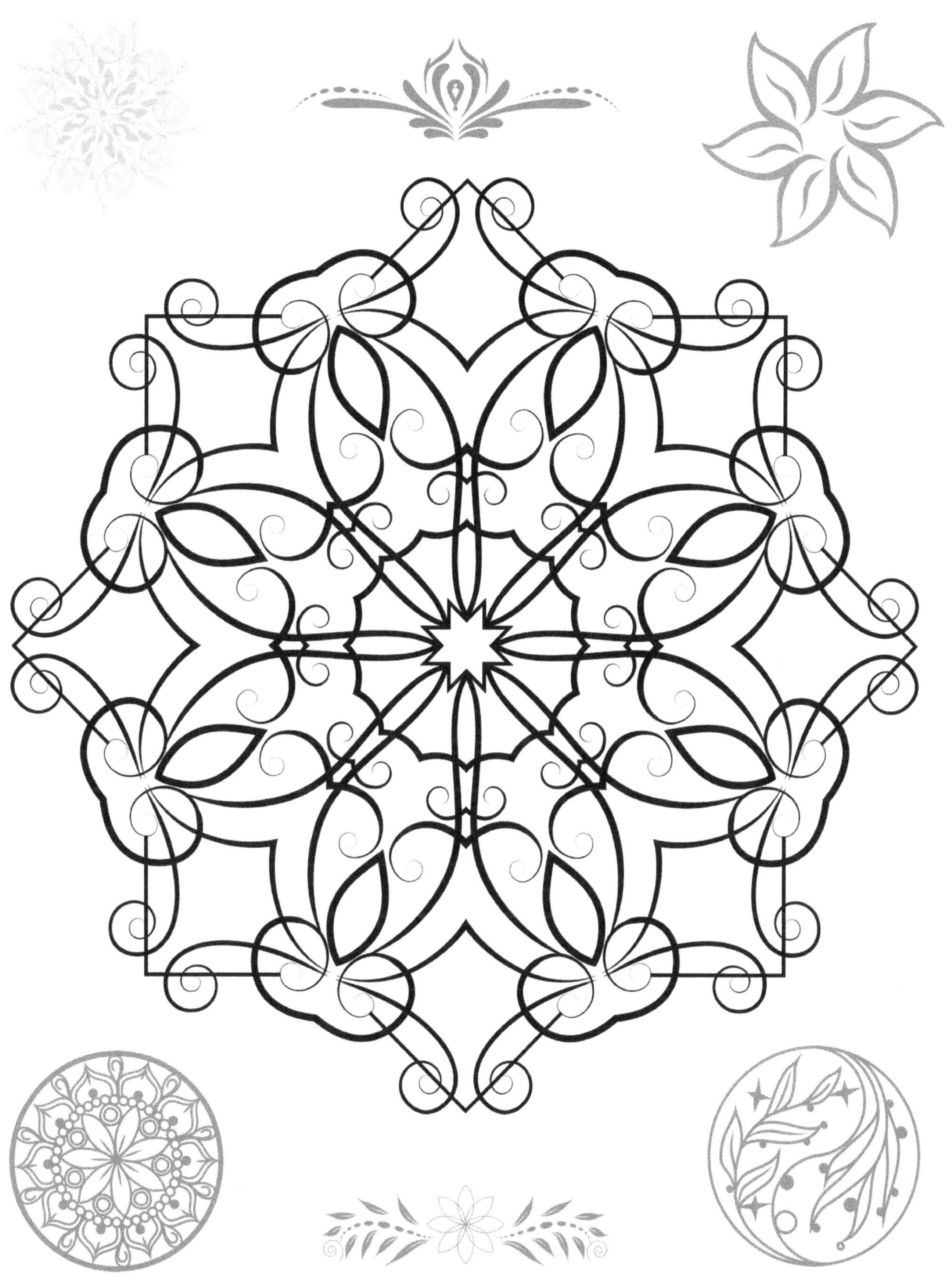

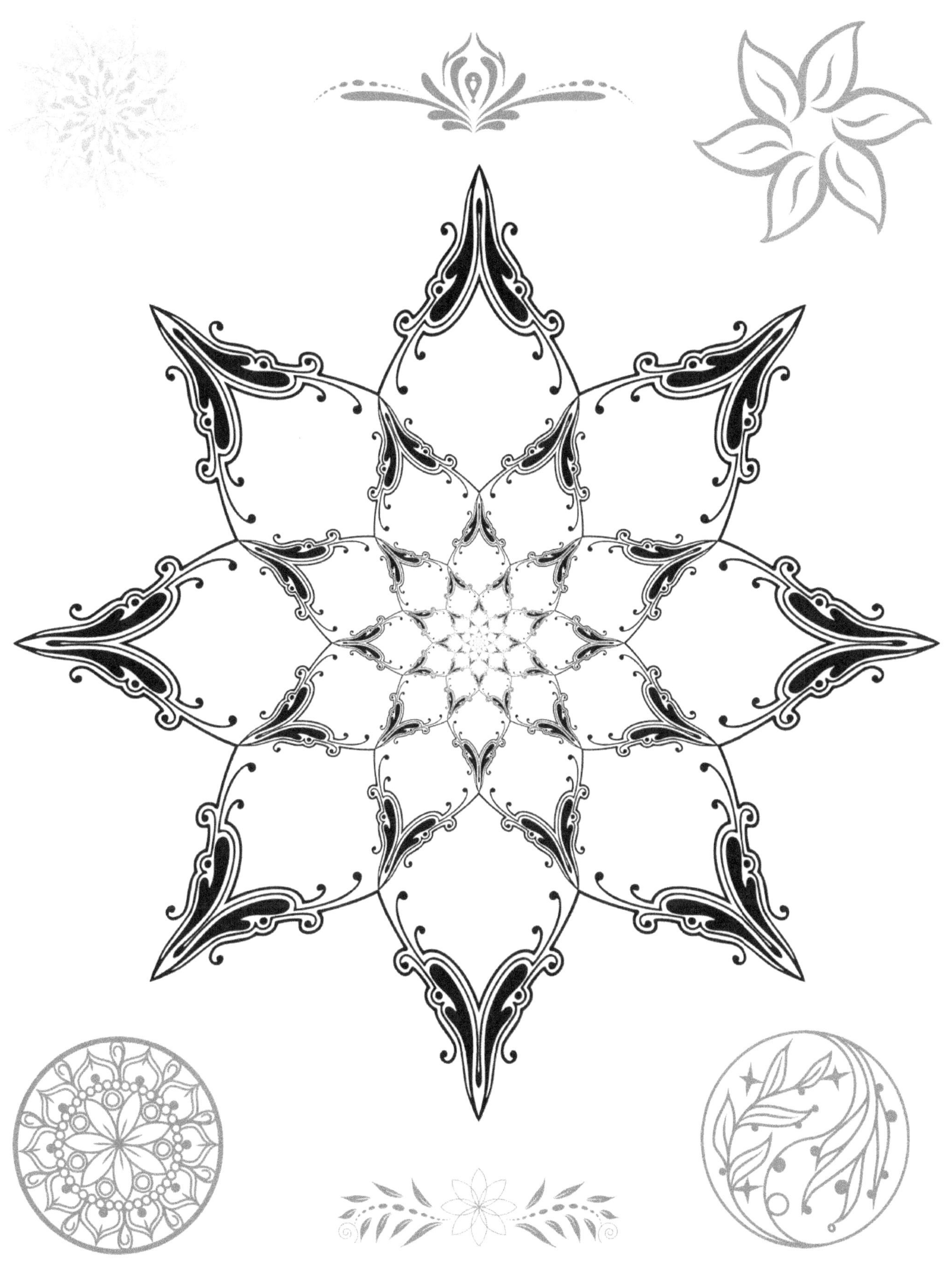

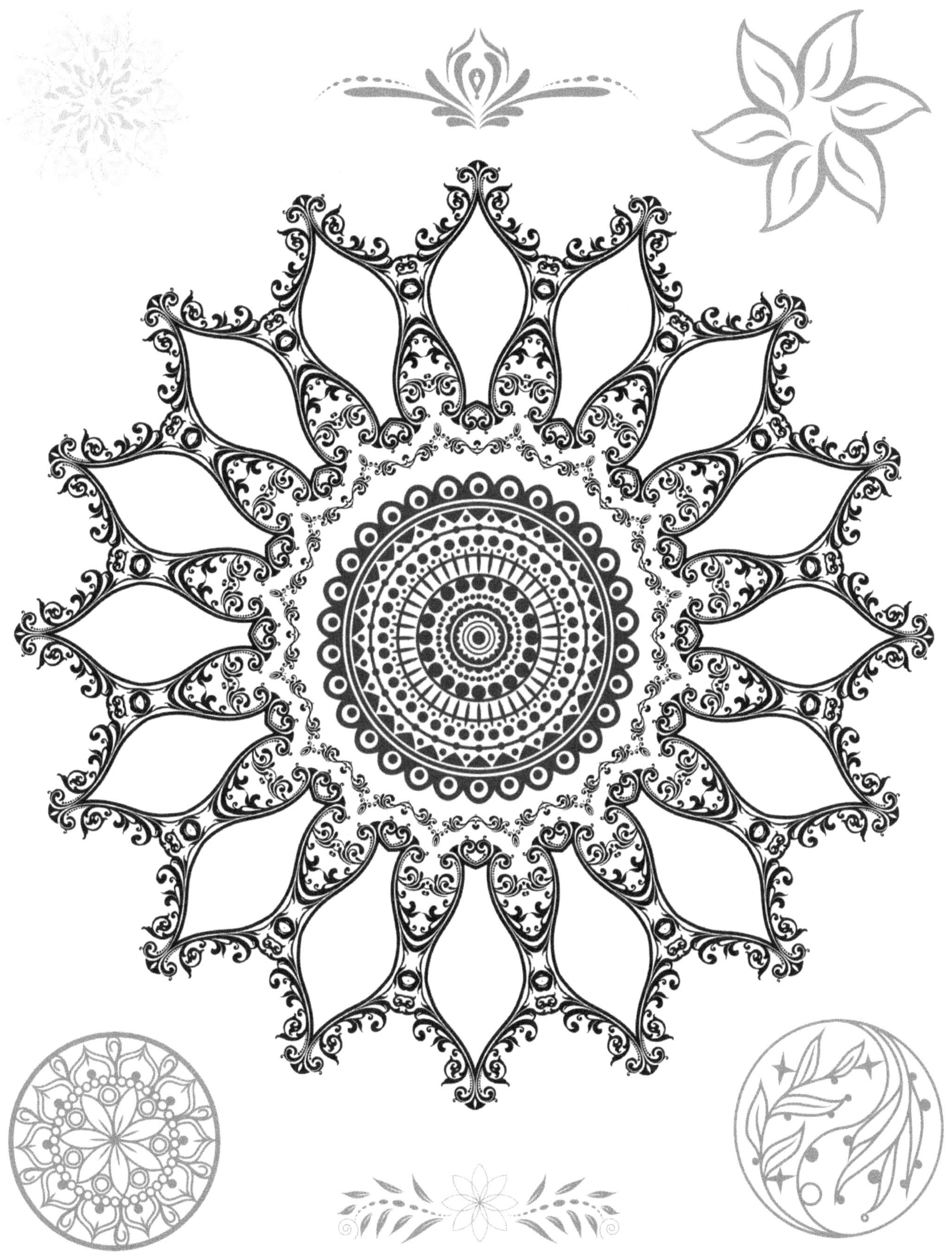

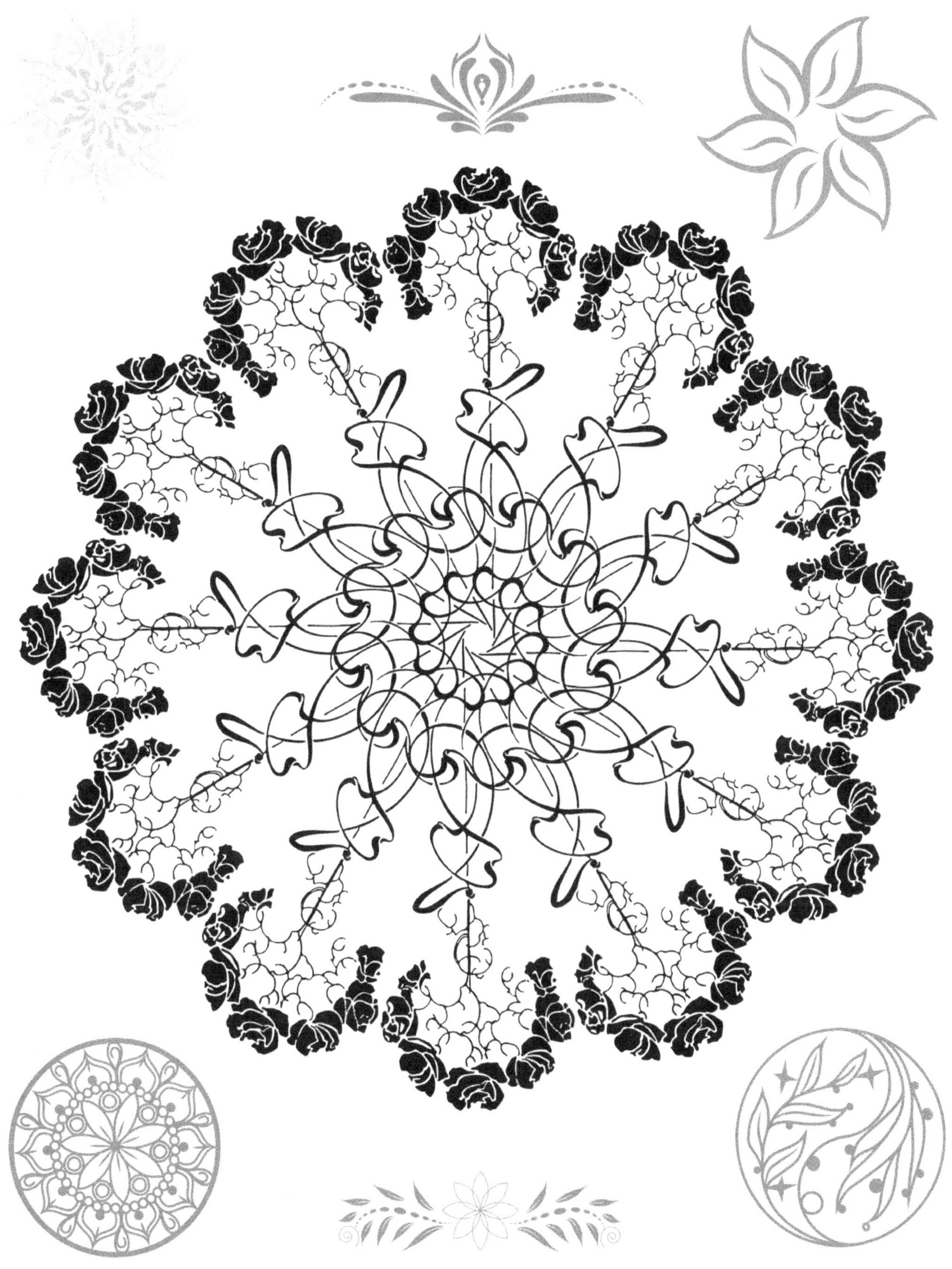

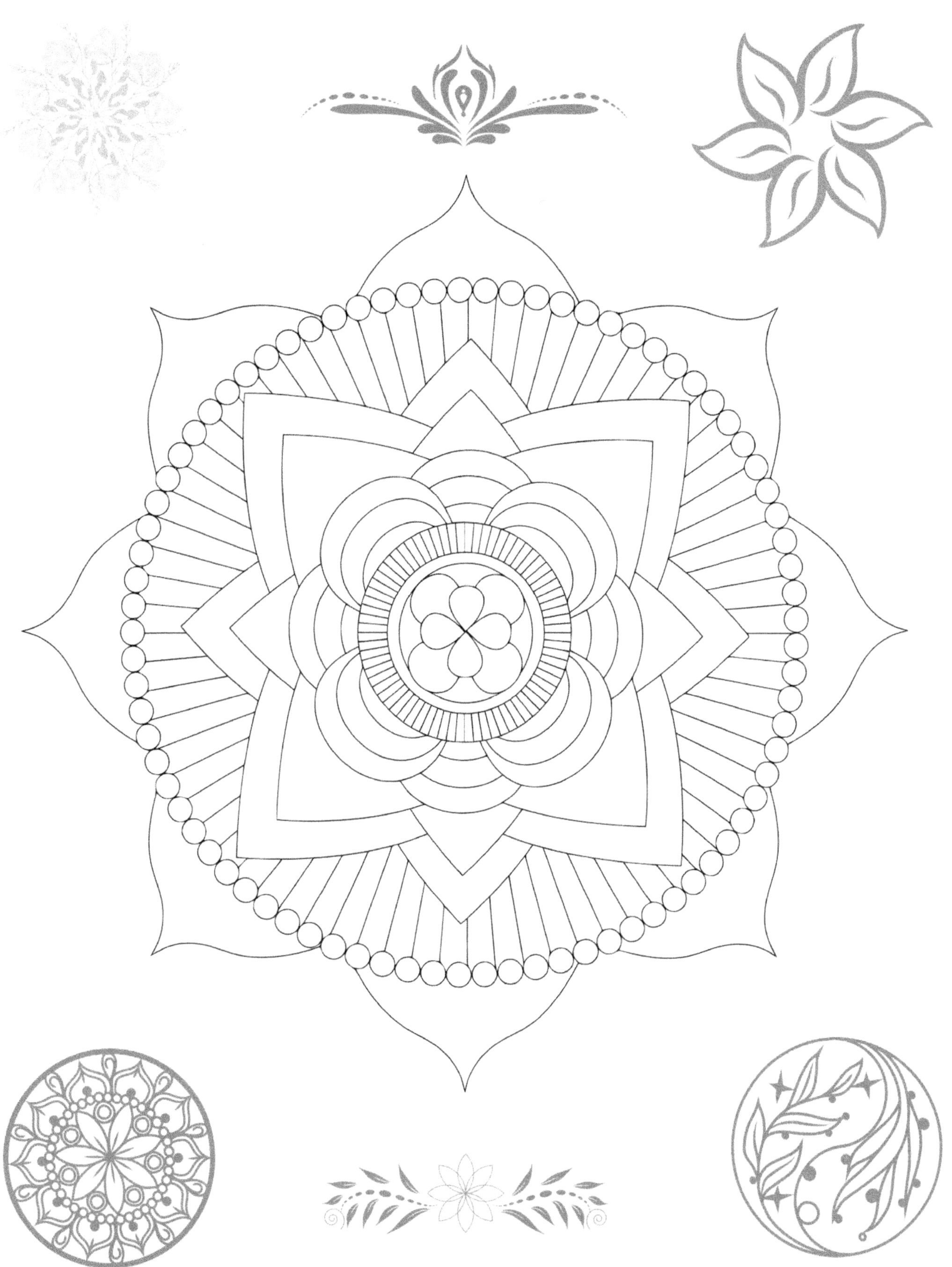

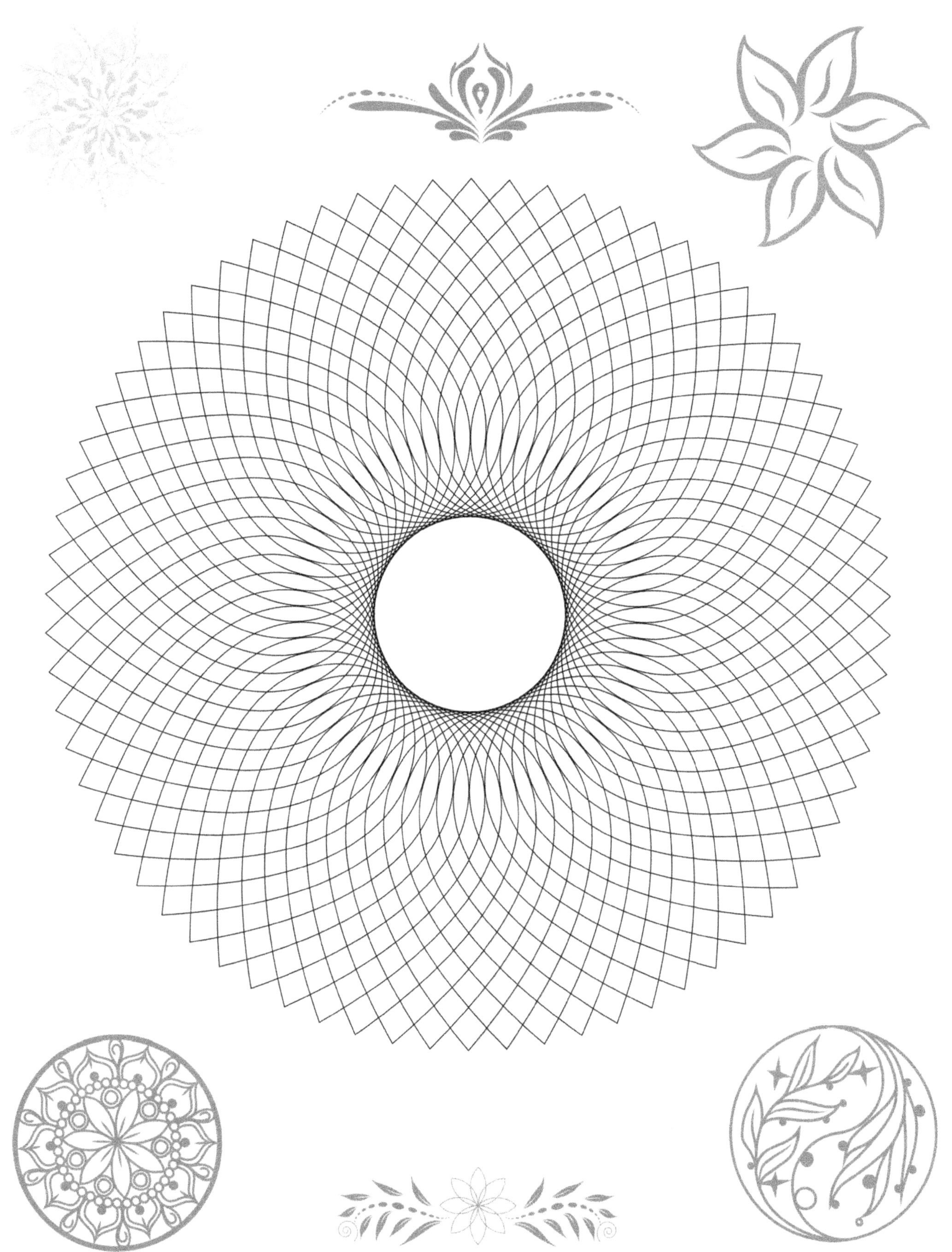

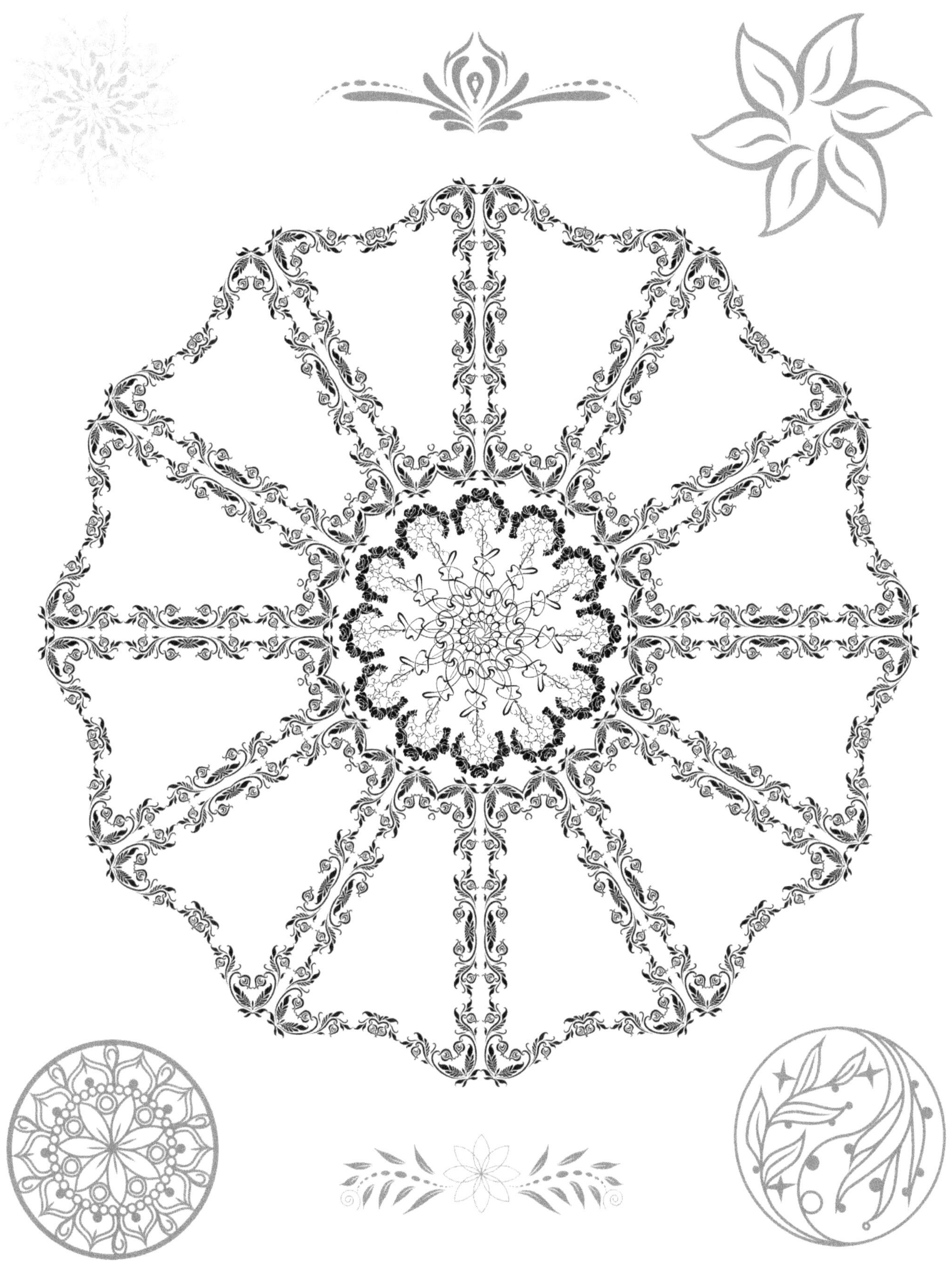

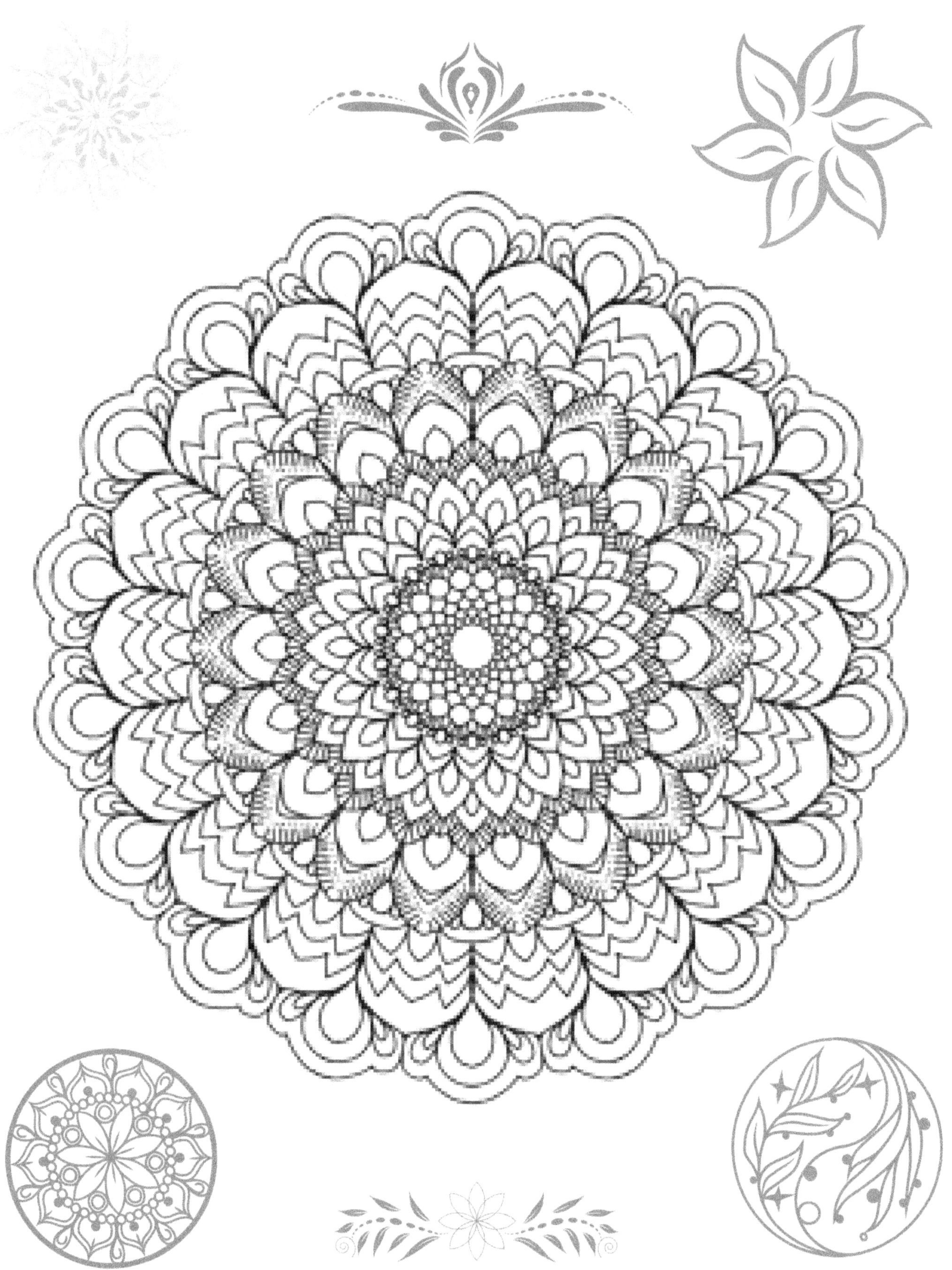

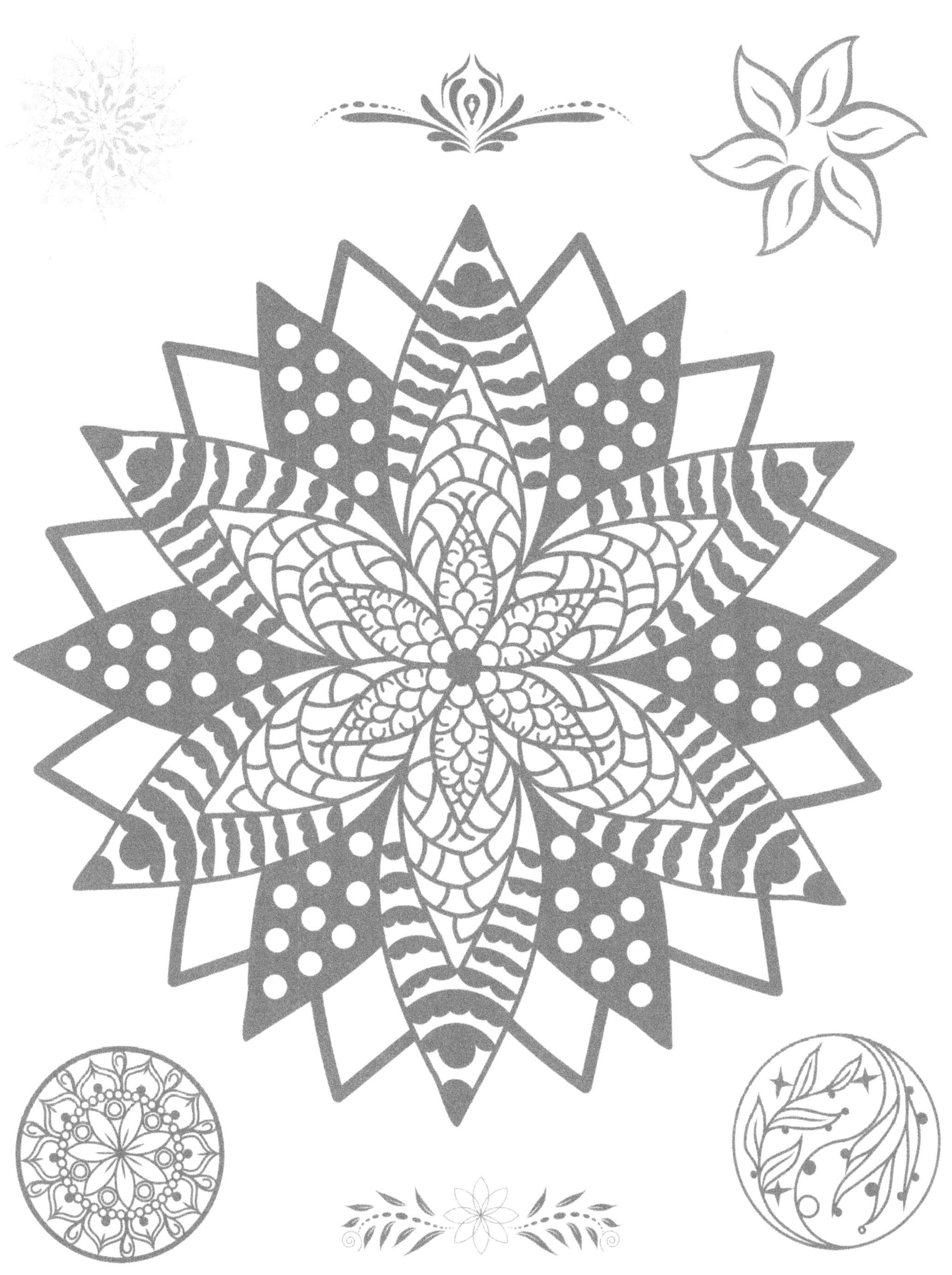

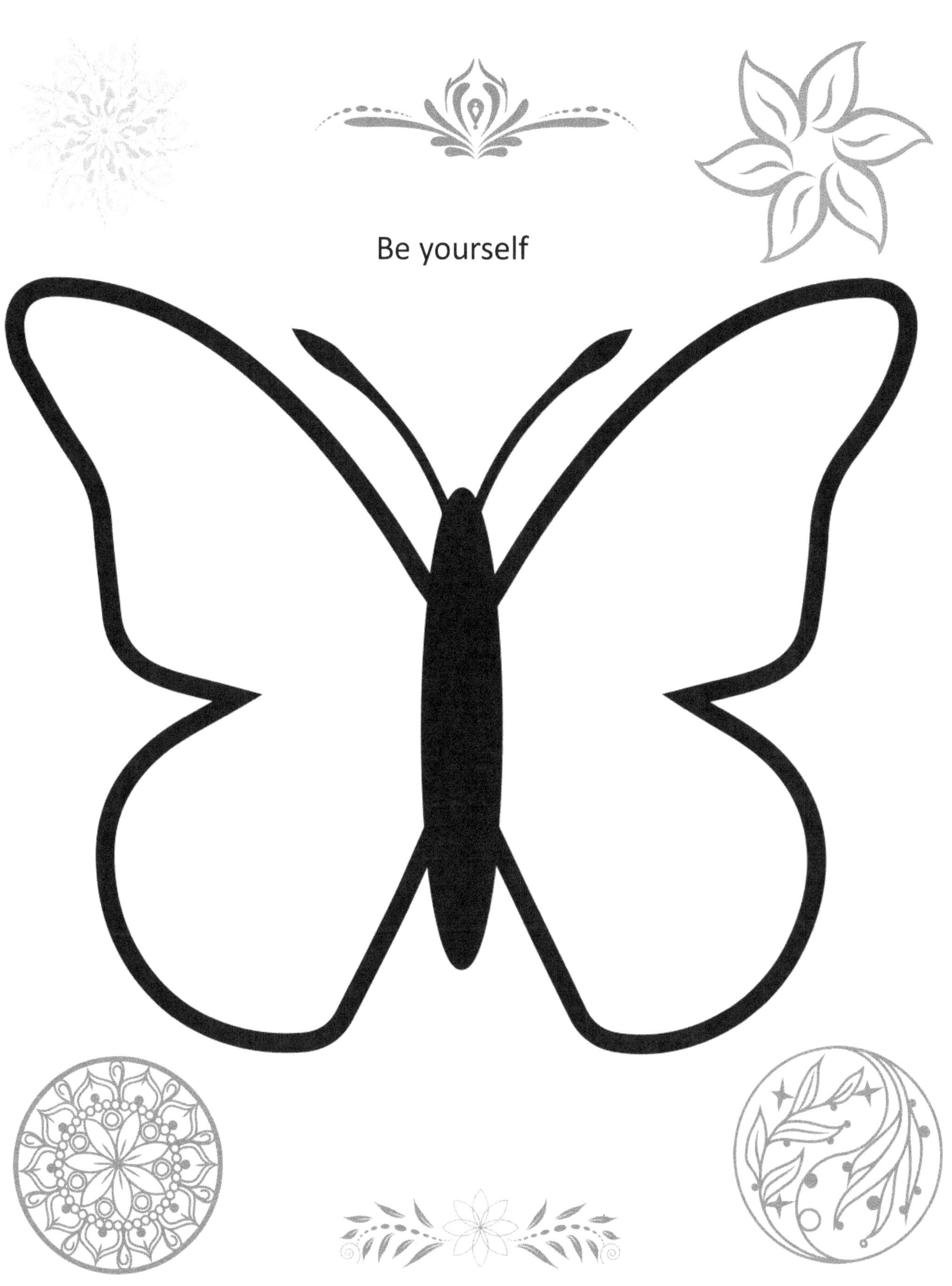
Be yourself

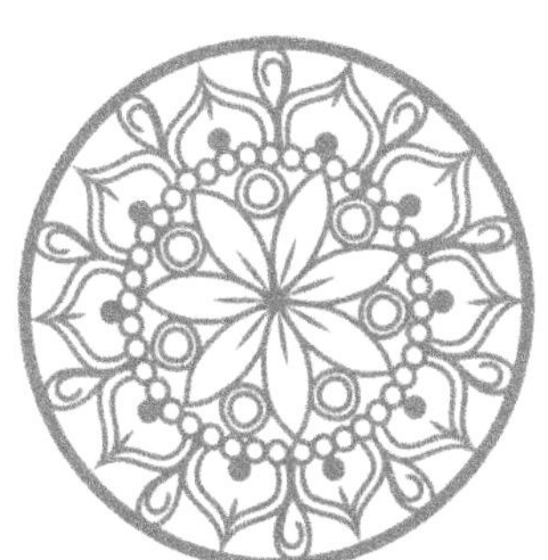

Thank you for showing your talent.

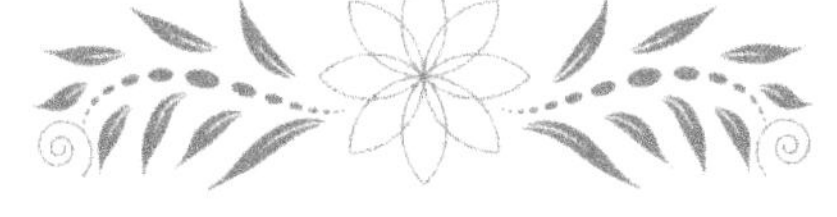

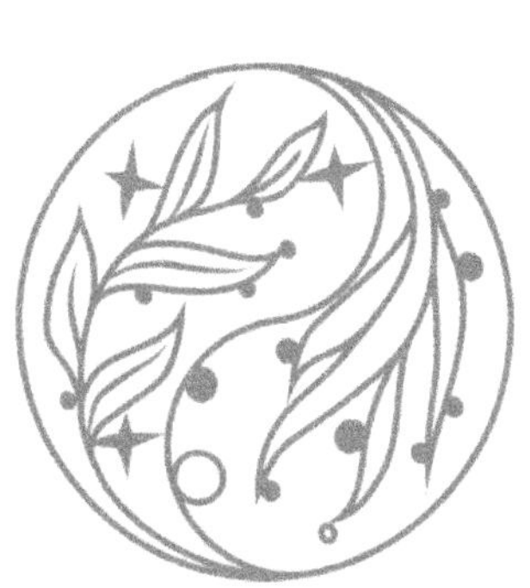

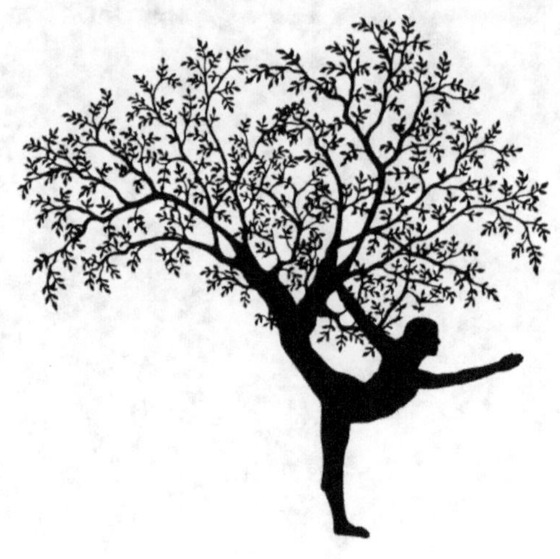